Sarah Tytler

The Huguenot Family

Vol. 1

Sarah Tytler

The Huguenot Family
Vol. 1

ISBN/EAN: 9783337292447

Printed in Europe, USA, Canada, Australia, Japan

Cover: Foto ©Lupo / pixelio.de

More available books at **www.hansebooks.com**

THE
HUGUENOT FAMILY.

VOL. I.

THE

HUGUENOT FAMILY.

BY

SARAH TYTLER

AUTHOR OF

"CITOYENNE JACQUELINE,"
&c. &c.

IN THREE VOLUMES.

VOL. I.

LONDON:
HURST AND BLACKETT, PUBLISHERS,
13, GREAT MARLBOROUGH STREET.
1867.

LONDON:
PRINTED BY MACDONALD AND TUGWELL, BLENHEIM HOUSE,
BLENHEIM STREET, OXFORD STREET.

TO

Elspeth

OF WHOM HER FRIENDS MUST THINK

BECAUSE SHE DOES NOT

THINK OF HERSELF

IN AFFECTIONATE ACKNOWLEDGMENT

OF ALL HER CARE AND KINDNESS

AND PURE SYMPATHY.

THE HUGUENOT FAMILY.

CHAPTER I.

Grand'mère Dupuy's opinion of the English.

"YOLANDE, my child, we must make friends with the people about us. I am desolate here without my children, my poor, who used to come to the châtelet and suffer themselves to be served on Saturday."

"If you are desolate, grand'mère, what are we? Why, you always remind me of the singing-birds which abound in this England, one of the few good things we have come so far to find."

"There is nothing common and unclean, my impatient grand-daughter; you ought to know better. 'Patient as a Huguenot' is a proverb, and all is fair to those who have the eyes to see it. As to the singing, I learned earlier than any of you to sing in a cage, and to what music!"

"I know, grand'mère. It was to the sound of threats and curses, and the volleys of the dragonnades. You were one of the children imprisoned and tormented in order to turn you from the faith, which you kept, good grand'mère, because 'out of the mouths of babes and sucklings God has perfected praise.'"

"Ah! the babes and sucklings know little better what they are saying, and have no more merit of will and choice than the Innocents. When they have will and choice, how they falter and fall away, because the flesh is weak."

"But, grand'mère, I do not know, and perhaps it is audacious to say it, but it seems to me the hot persecution which lasted but a moment, because no living creatures, in their nature, could endure it longer, was not so much harder to bear than life—long exile and isolation among strangers and foreigners who hate us and slander us, grand'mère."

"They do not all hate us, little one, though their Defoe has written,

> 'Two hundred thousand pairs of wooden shoes,
> Who, God be thank'd, had nothing left to lose;'

and 'no longer strangers and foreigners,' was once written to men more hunted and despised than ever we or our fathers have been. 'All things are easy,' but troubles are best not talked of, at least they are talked of enough by your mother, who did not live near enough to the worst of them to feel that they could not really hurt—just as we shall feel death cannot hurt us one day, though it has been our *bête noire* all our lives. Just so are troubles when we look back and count what they have cost without experiencing the blessing and the joy of the persecuted. In the same way you would grudge to be still paying by instalments the price of my wedding gown, of which you never saw the beauty, and which was unpicked, and cut down, and made anew into a mantle for my son Hubert, forty years before you were born. But you have not the excuse of your mother, Yolande; you never saw the sun of France, nor worshipped in a *Temple*, under a pastor of your own people—a sufferer like yourself among fellow sufferers; nor did you ever go a-marketing in the old *Place*, or pull great gourds, red and yellow like the sunset, or gather caper blossom, scented with vanille. You have nothing to complain of; you are English born, and can speak the English tongue like a native; you are a true Englishwoman."

"Never, grand'mère, I would rather be—Catholic."

"Hush! I shall tell you what you are—a French Jew. All the nationalities which think themselves better than the other nationalities are Jewish, and all the Churches which think themselves better than the other Churches are Jewish. But at the same time I beg the pardon of the poor Jews for the comparison. They had reason for their exclusiveness, while the French and the English, Roman Catholic or Reformed, have none, and even profess to have none. For me, I love France; I do not say how I love France: I think of her every day, dream of her every night, till I am tempted to be an idolatress, and to imagine that Heaven will be like the native country. And, indeed, so it will be in one sense, Yolande, for it is the Father's house. The French know what that means to a marvel, though one has told me that it is used as a reproach against them, that they have no turn of phrase save 'with myself,' or 'my household,' for what the English call 'sweet home.' The French have the Father's house, at least. But as for me, I am charmed with England—it is so like Holland, and is so cool and fresh in this bit of meadow land. With the English rudeness and truth also, which reminds me of the prickly bosquets of roses I once reared in my garden, where M. Claude had walked. These English have had their own way ever since they killed their king, which was very wicked—indeed, quite profane. The French have done nothing of the kind, though the unhappy Charles, misled by his mother and his brother, and by Guise and Lorraine, fired from the Louvre on his people on that night of despair, when our Coligni, a very lion at bay, was slain; and our Henry of Navarre—Jeanne d'Albret's brave boy—was held a prisoner. The 'religion' in its professors has always regarded it as one of the most cruel and calumnious accusations brought against 'the faithful' that they were not loyal. It is only madmen and assassins, like Clement and Ravaillac, who would slay the Lord's anointed. But from that day to this the English have had their own way; and have they abused it? No. They have had a few thousands of bread-rioters, breakers of our French machinery, and burners of the houses of Catholics, it is true; but there will always be doubtful characters in every class and nation. The brave, patient people have been quiet and tolerant, just and merciful. The English have been masters in their parliaments and on their battle-fields, since the man of the people, Oliver—not the barber, Yolande, the brewer, and oh! such another brewer, a hero who spoke brave words, mighty words for the oppressed Vaudois, our brethren in Piedmont, and behold the honour! The English have kept their heads. They have not been gasconaders, or tyrants of the *canaille*, undoing themselves and others. I believe that in their noble, savage way they have given God the glory. I esteem, I honour, I salute the English, not only for the shelter they afford us, poor driven dust of emigrants, but for the example they present of possessing their own big souls in patience."

"Well, grand'mère, I wish they returned the compliment. I cannot see, for my part, that the admiration and the friendship should all be on one side."

"Ah! then you do not see the wellspring of Christian life which burst from the broken heart of the Divine Founder. But this monopoly you speak of, as one would of the salt-tax in France, is what I began our conversation by scolding about. I don't want to limit the love of one's neighbour to me and my house. Not at all. I want to have it everywhere, like the good air we breathe; but I must show my good-will in order to win a sight of another's good-will. I believe it is present even throughout the universe, north and south, east and west, among great multitudes of every kindred and tongue and nation, only it is hidden from us; and we traverse each the other's streets, and rub each the other's clothes, not knowing each other—bah !— but elbowing each other and knitting our brows at each other. Now, I desire that we should know each other better here at Sedge Pond. We came here before the buds were on the trees; at present they are in full leaf, and I have not yet made a friend of a living creature in the place, save the birds, the cats, and the dogs. I shall pass over the sheep, the oxen, and the horses, and go on at once to the poor, my children, at Toulouse, whom I have missed more than the green leaves, and the warbling, purring, barking voices of friends in London. No; London is not a modern Babylon, as your mother calls it, it is a great Christian city, full of violence and excess and selfish luxury, but also alive with brave battlings for truth and justice and noble wants, like our own Paris. It may be rolled in blood and bathed in fire, but it is no more Babylon than the Lord's gospel is the law of Moses. Our Paris and this London cannot perish and be given over to obscene beasts; because they are redeemed with a price—in Christ first, and then in all their righteous men, sublime martyrs, and returned prodigals, in every century, following afar off, after Him, in endless conqueror's procession. The Christian cities will come out pure as the gold, glad as the light in their day. But the question with us just now is, not of great London, but of little Sedge Pond; and the little one is not to be despised, since it may need us the most. I shall set about learning to know the people, or rather, for I flatter myself I know them a little already, teaching the people to know me, Grand'mére Dupuy, of the Shottery Cottage, countrywoman and sister of good Vincent de Paul, though he acknowledge me not; and I command you to help me, Yolande."

The speaker was a little old woman, dressed in a Lyons silk gown, with the skirt drawn through the pocket holes. She wore a mob cap of fine lace, had mittens on her hands, and her neckerchief was fastened by a silver dove instead of a cross. She was at that moment resting on a staff, with a carved coral head, representing another little old woman in scarlet. Her rustling silk, her cobweb lace, her foreign accent, and

and her lovely old face might have clearly told the onlooker that she belonged to the latter part of the last century, and to that country which owns at once the loveliest and the ugliest old women. The accessories, too, suited the main figure. The room had an air of quiet, but was not without its ornaments. There was an elaborately decorated and festooned bed in one corner; a curtain hung before the door; a wood-fire was on the hearth; and there were on the walls a few foreign prints, mostly of gaunt, careworn men, in Geneva gowns and skull-caps. Her companion was a tall, slender girl of sixteen, in as rustling a silk gown and as heavy a quilted petticoat as the old lady's. She had a little cap on her head, which surmounted a roll of black-brown hair. The girl's face was prematurely womanly, and delicately cut, bearing a resemblance to her relative's, though with less colour, and more shaded and sharp than the old woman's could ever have been; but it was a sort of paraphrase of the old woman's beauty, sicklied over, hollowed, and worn betimes, by the fact of its having blossomed in the shade, carrying, before it was able to carry it, a burden of thought. The big eyes had taken a grave, far-withdrawn, unfathomable look, from their striving to read the enigma of a sinning, suffering world, without their owner's having got the key of faith, or while the key, still but a wax model, took, but did not retain, the shape of any obstacle to which it was applied, in place of combating and overcoming it.

CHAPTER II.

Grand'mère Dupuy's attempt to make friends with the people about her.

GRAND'MÈRE DUPUY was a resolute, enthusiastic old woman, and was no cipher, but a ruling spirit, though it must be understood that she ruled with the old metaphorical ivory wand, draped in myrtle, in the house of her married, middle-aged emigrant son. Accordingly, that very afternoon, as she had said, she set about beginning her attack upon what she had found the locked and padlocked fortresses of Britons' hearts at Sedge Pond.

With innocent wile and womanly tact she said to Yolande,

"These honest villagers hunger, though they do not starve, as they did in poor France after its bloody wars and ghastlier splendours. Yes, these Sedge Pond folk want in the midst of plenty. They live, like the hogs, on sodden bread, raw meat, and vegetables. They have the dyspepsia or the spleen. See how purple and tallow-faced they are; hear of their surfeits, their fevers, their wastes, their pinings. They really know nothing of their own word 'comfort,' save in connection with swilling and smoking in the ale-house. That is not even a resting-place for travellers, as with us,—only a rendezvous for the natives. When we are merry, it is under the walnut and olive-trees, in the games. It may be giddiness and light-mindedness, as your mother says; but it is not riot. But when they are merry, it is in the ale-house—always the ale-house. Even when they have the fair, what is it but the whole streets filled, the stalls surrounded, the caravans visited by the customers of the ale-house? The marriage-guests are borrowed from the ale-house; their harvest-feasts are kept in the ale-house, or are versions of the ale-house feasts in granaries and barns. Fie! I believe their magistrates sit, their choristers practise, their clerks, perhaps even their ministers, relax themselves from their cock-fighting and their execution of highwaymen in the ale-house. In one word, comfort and amusement for the peasants of England mean—the ale-house. My child, the stomach has something to do with that; the cooking, the house-keeping at least, may be improved. I don't say that we have not a great deal to learn ourselves, above all a marmot, a flower of the cabbage like you, Yolande; but we will remember that wherever the French have settled the leprosy and the scurvy have disappeared. We will let the poor people taste our savoury *pot-à-feu,* our cool *goûter* of the sliced artichoke or the cucumber, our warm *ragoût* of the cutlets or the kidneys, our bland almond milk and our sweet succory water. I wager they never tasted anything so nice, and will not care for the harsh heady yeast after it. They will turn their backs on the ale-house and its commodities. We will go to-day to Goody Gubbins; she is an incurable, and has only the parish for her relations. I have seen the pastor's servants carrying her greasy messes and muddy slops, just a little better than the everlasting beans and bacon and hunches of bread and cheese of the ale-house. Who knows but, if the good God will bless the deed, we may work a Reformed miracle, and heal the sick?"

Madame Dupuy's intentions were excellent and kindly, though a little short-sighted and halting, as the most excellent intentions of fallible mortals are apt to be. But she did not let the grass grow beneath her ancient, tripping, high-heeled, silver-buckled feet in executing them. She had her own cooking apparatus and her own stores: ingenious though economical the one, and of an ample, skilful range the other. She was never without her simmering *pot-à-feu*, the materials for her summer or winter *goûter*, or the glass in which her pebbles of sugar were dissolving and sinking in a thick, luscious syrup to the bottom of the clear spring water. She had her pipkins, her ewers, her trays—plain enough, for she had come from among a people who were so staunch that not more than a third of their number had succumbed in creed to a lengthened era of fines, penalties, imprisonments, and law-suits, which had converted their silver to copper, and their porcelain to earthenware. But all the utensils were distinguished by clever fitness for their end, by neatness of form and gaiety of tone, and when the austerity into which the Huguenot Church has been driven did not forbid it, even by an elegant simplicity of design. Nor did it detract much from the elegant simplicity of Grand'-mère Dupuy's accompaniments that in practice she wore silk and lace, or that in principle she was a Huguenot and *bourgeoise*. M. Dupuy had been and was still connected in trade with silk manufactures; and no one, with any pretensions to the position of a gentlewoman, dressed in other materials at that date. On close inspection it might have been seen that the silk had been very artistically scoured, and the lace very artistically darned. And on minor matters again, Madame Dupuy was more of a French woman, and still more of a human being, than anything else.

After dinner Grand'mère Dupuy set out from the Shottery Cottage with Yolande, who carried the *pot-à-feu* in a pipkin moulded from a gourd, with a gourd leaf and stalk for the handle, and carried it very much as another girl would have carried a basket of roses, or a casket of jewels; but still sombrely, distrustfully, reluctantly, for all her air. Grand'mère walked slowly beside her with her coral-headed staff, eagerly recounting, as she went, how she had always taken it with her when she went to visit her sick at Toulouse, until the peasants hailed it, made much of it, named it the little red madame, Madame Rougeole.

The village of Sedge Pond at any period in the eighteenth century was by no means a model village. It was situated between London and Norwich. All was misty, flat, and monotonous about it; but there was the perfection of verdure in marsh and meadow, broken only by patches of yellow-bearded corn and red-flowered clover. There was a sleepy, lulling motion in the slow river, with its clumsy barges, and there was breadth in the blue distance. The roads, both high-road and by-road, were heavily rutted in their yellow soil; the low-lands were liable to be flooded at particular seasons by the sluggish, stagnant brown water. There were rough, bristling, purple and olive-coloured bits of " wääste " to take in everywhere. There was a castle—a mass of pretentious white masonry, which had replaced a more picturesque, weather-stained, crumbling tower, partly seen among the woods which rose above the Dupuys' cottage; and there was a rectory like a château itself, steep-roofed, gabled, and pinnacled, and with pleasure-grounds, and a wilderness. This latter had the advantage of a constant tenant and a numerous, flourishing household. There was not another good house in the village, saving Shottery Cottage, which was a remote appendage of the castle, and the ale-house, which was a place of public entertainment, and not of private convenience. The other houses stood in irregular rows and groups, and were dropsical, bulged-out, discoloured cottages, covered with thatch, and in every stage of rottenness. For that matter they were much indebted to the house-leek, and here and there to a side growth of ivy, for holding them together; for nature was trying hard to embroider them over with some of her own leaf and flower-work—wonderfully good embroidery, which makes men forget the ruin in rapture at the tracery over it. There were no spouts above, nor gutters below the cottages, nothing to protect them from the prevailing wet except narrow stone ledges, like eyelids without eyelashes, placed above the never-opened windows, filled with small, thick, diamond-shaped panes of glass, where they were not broken and boarded up, or stuffed with straw, grass, wool, or anything which had at the moment come to hand. Beyond these ledges the moisture dripped, soaked, gathered, and grew green-coated. The common was a puddle, the wells were one or two open draw-wells, and before each door there was a heap of fermenting, festering refuse. Any gardens belonging to the cottages were like the villagers in this respect, that their good qualities were out of sight. They lay in diminutive shaggy plots of potatoes, turnips, herbs, with occasionally a straggling, neglected, and misused flower, hidden behind the houses. Indeed, had it not been for the quiet, home-like landscape, with its corn-fields in their cool fresh green, ripening and whitening in strips and nooks among the pasture, and the castle park thrusting forward and separating the more rural scene with a woodland bluff or shoulder, dark with tufts of chestnuts, oaks, and plane-trees, the village of Sedge Pond would have been as uncomely a village as ever housed refugees, and bred and fostered small-pox, purple fever, and ague.

The church was half a mile distant from the village, which was thus out of the comfortable sight of its spire, and of everything but the faint sound of its hoarse bell, although it was easily reached, down a short lane communicating by a private gate, about midway up the castle avenue. The little churchyard, in one visitation of the plague, had become full to the brim, and the oppressed earth—crammed not by means of coffins, but by trenches—had been forced up breast high with the wall, and was left behind, to add its quota to the other disease-distilling influences of Sedge Pond.

In some eyes the ale-house atoned for all defects and drawbacks. It was a low, wide, octagonal building of mellow red brick, with stone coping, and containing several large, low-browed, brown rooms, with long tables, wattled seats and benches, and in which there were fires at every season, smouldering like carbuncles, or roaring and blazing like furnaces. These were the chosen retreats from the skittle-ground, the bowling-green, and the court where the mains between the game-cocks were fought on each side of the white-washed porch. All the revelry and debauchery of the neighbourhood went on there; and revelry and debauchery were so much the gross habit of the day, that the place set apart for them was not viewed with any suspicion, but was actually invested with an influence and respectability which absolved it from the necessity of becoming the "Castle Arms," or seeking such patronage as any tavern, inn, or hostelry in the kingdom would now do. If one takes into account, in addition, the white foam of tankards, the light curling blue vapour of pipes, the cribbage boards, the soiled newsletters for those who desired other stimulants and more intellectual influences, together with the social intercourse, and occasionally the larger gatherings of a more festive character, where there was a mixture of sexes, it is possible to understand how to the hob-nailed, red-cloaked peasants of Sedge Pond, comfort and amusement meant the ale-house. What Grand'mère Dupuy had therefore to contend with, when she proposed to supersede their staple good, with its black shadow of brutality and crime, was something which would sorely task her light, subtle French substitutes, unless she supplemented them by something infinitely better.

Goody Gubbins' cottage was the worst in its row. There, on straw and rags, with chronic damp chilling her rheumatic, palsied limbs, and without daylight to cheer her, her life was barely kept in by the Church's dole, although otherwise she lay quite uncared for and unsolaced, her body begrimed and engrained with dirt, and her grizzled hair matted beneath her filthy linen curch— a wreck of humanity.

But Grand'mère Dupuy, of the Church under the Cross, recognised humanity under any aspect, and had no quarrel with it. There was nothing in her but self-reproachfulness and self-forgetfulness, struggling for mastery, and, overpowering both, a mother's and a sister's tenderness. It was Yolande who revolted and shrank from the disfigured, disguised old woman, for the keen French analysis, which records " how severe are the young," reads in various ways.

"Good day, my friend," began Grand'-mère, "I am afraid you are very ailing, but you will improve, and all your ills will vanish by-and-bye; if not here, hereafter," proceeded she, in her liquid, persuasive foreign accent, as she nodded now and then emphatically. "We have taken the liberty, and given ourselves the pleasure of bringing you some soup," continued Grand'mère, coming to the gist of her discourse, and gathering up her hooped skirt cleverly as she advanced lightly (that is, lightly for her fourscore years) to the side of the bed or lair, the better to aid her pet of an old woman to receive her refreshment.

Goody had been dosing when the Dupuys invaded her hovel, and in the dim light and the gathering mists of age, ignorance, stupidity, and suffering, she might well have looked scared as well as mazed when she was aroused to the unwonted and unaccountable apparition. "Who be you?" she gasped, clutching her torn coverlet, and staring at her visitors in blind hostility as well as blank wonder. "A dunna know you—you be seeking summat of a poor lorn body. A's nought to give or to tell. How should a?" she moaned out, her moaning mixed with a loud whimper of protest.

The reception was not encouraging, but Grand'mère was patient.

"We are two of the French family at Shottery Cottage, women like yourself, my good dame, and we have heard of your infirmities. Ah, dear Lord!—that they have been sorely neglected so long. We have come to succour you and ease them; not to serve ourselves, save by serving you."

Goody Gubbins had not heard of very many things, but she had heard of the

French, to fight against whom stout village lads of her acquaintance had enlisted as soldiers under Wolfe or Cornwallis, and marched from their villages, not one in ten of them ever to see their native land again. Naturally she looked on the French as her mortal enemies, and when she heard that the two women were members of the French family who had penetrated into the village, through the recklessness of the lords of the castle, to get round her and entrap her, bedridden and pauper as she was, she set up a screech of utmost dismay and virulent opposition.

"Noa, noa! Pearson! Neebour Clay! —help!—help! A'm flayed! a'm murdered! though a never flapped, or clemmed, or so much as set eye on French maid or man before a took to my bed—not when a were the strappingest wife and wench in the parish. Alack-a-day!"

"You deceive yourself, you are in error; rest quiet. Try the soup, my dear." And Grand'mère, in the difficulty, popped the uncovered pipkin right below Goody's nose.

Goody Gubbins had not been called "my dear" since the day when her good man was lying in intermittent fever, induced by draughts of the over-ripe October of which he died, thus paying the penalty of his eight-and-forty hours' sojourn at the alehouse, drinking the health of the German George, who had come to be king in the room of good Queen Anne. She did not take well with the epithet; it made her grue just as when Giles Gubbins was first "soft" with her, to get her harvest wages out of her pocket, and the lawful means failing, then beat her black and blue, and obtained his end unlawfully, save that it was in his character of a husband. But the smell of this rich *omnium gatherum*, which had boiled and bubbled till it had refined itself of everything but the very core of good things, was more fragrant than the gales of Araby the Blest to the stunted, blunted nostrils. She sniffed and coughed, and sniffed again, and her patriotism and prejudices wavered.

"There bean't snails in it?" she inquired, tremulously, her toothless chops watering, her bleared eyes blinking greedily.

"Not one. It is the very best of soups, my good woman; the true soup for an invalid, while you have been swallowing—ouf!—hard roots, dry seeds of grain, grease and water."

"The broth and the bit of flesh is none so bad as you make it, be yourn what it like." Goody began to speak up for her food, offended, like her betters, that her right of grumbling should be appropriated by a stranger and foreigner. "If Pearson's Sam and Sally weren't so long on the way, and didn't go to spill it at the stile, and have their share of it off their long fingers. There bean't toads in it?" pausing with revived jealousy, after she had ventured to taste and dwell on a mouthful.

"No, no; faith of Geneviève Dupuy. But why do you object to the poor, soft, fat, white fellows of snails, when you do not refuse to eat the raw bleeding flesh. The mourgettes are very good for the sick," remonstrated Madame, with rash innocence; "for the frogs, I can tell you they are not so easy to get here," she reflected, pensively.

"Lawks! there would be if she could get em!" declared the old woman, stiffening like stone and dropping the spoon. "Noa, noa, it's pisen, it's witches' broo; the corns of barley and the peas ne'er grit agin my single tooth; a did not taste ingens; it's like nought on earth but balm wine and the smell of the dogs' messes up at the castle. Get ye gone! a wunna swallow another drop of the broo, a've telled 'ee, a'll swound, a'll be throttled first!" cried Goody, in a renewed paroxysm of terror and rage, and thrust her rags into her mouth with all the force which remained to her claw-like hands.

So there was nothing for it but for Grand'mère to retreat before the misled maddened object of her charity should fulfil her threat.

"You see, Grand'mère," observed Yolande significantly.

"She does not know what is good for her, the poor suspicious, straitened heart. Yolande, you would not be so mean and foolish as to resent what a poor miserable creature imagines to her injury," Grand'mère said, more reproachfully than usual—indeed, almost with severity—to her grand-daughter. Then she turned and began to blame herself sharply, which was much more in her way, and a safer course for reformers. "We are punished because we have begun at the wrong end. We ought to have addressed ourselves to the little ones, and made friends of them first. Look, they run wild, or they are toilers from their cradles, poor broken-backed, gloomy-looking gamins and cocottes, and they grow up totally without knowledge. I do not believe there are six men and women among the peasants of Sedge Pond can read and write. The school of the pastor is for the sons and daughters of the farmers who can pay, the little boys and girls in little coats and collars, aprons and hoods —the country *bourgeoisie*, in fact. The pastor himself does not encourage the little peasants to come to the school; he says it teaches them conceit and disrespect to their superiors. I heard him say so in a sermon on useless acquirements and false pretences, at the church. But what teaching must that have been! Even the Jesuit fathers and the convent sisters would have taught better than that. My child, we will have a little class. Betty Sykes, Teddy Jones, Pierce and Bab Frew (I pick up the names as quickly as a magpie), will come, and you will instruct them in English reading, and I shall manage the writing and the figures, and we will make them wise—not foolish, and modest—not insolent. We will not tire of it, Butterfly, because it may not be so charming the second day as the first. We will work and weary, and work again, with the stolid little souls, because it will be our sowing for the world's harvest; and I tell you, Yolande, we will have fêtes and recompenses if your mother does not forbid them as vain and worldly."

Yolande was not sanguine. Indeed there was no sanguineness in the girl. All high hope was the portion of the old woman, who had fathomed adversity and knew how little it could hurt of itself, if men and women were truly armed against it. But Yolande was docile, and followed where Grand'mère led the way. So, with the Lyons silk tucked up, and the coral-headed staff, and with the companion silk without staff, the two went picking their way among the pools and the dirt-heaps, from door to door of the village, heavy with dense dulness, or only quickened here and there into rabid intolerance. They found every double-leafed, cut-across door literally and figuratively shut in their faces, and fared but poorly in their canvass for the school. One woman wanted her youngsters to watch the geese, feed the pig, break wood, draw water, as she had done in her own young days, and she thought they could not do better, or hope to master anything which would come more pat to their hands in after-life. The woman had right on her side. Madame assured her heartily these were very good things, admirable things, which were referred to as virtues and excellences in the book of Proverbs; but were they enough for gaining the victory over sin, for enlightening the understanding and disciplining the heart? Say, then, were they enough for that other life in the skies?

"Anan," answered Grand'mère's opponent. "She left all that to Pearson; that were his business, and weren't he paid for doing it? Poor bodies had enough to do to live, and fit their children to live, in these hard times."

Another speaker, a gruff man, who had been for years employed in the next manufacturing town, told Grand'mère that they wanted no creeping spies, nor crafty seducers, nor paid agents of the foreign cloth and silk weavers, no gunpowder and glass makers, who now swarmed in the land and preyed on it, and snatched the bite out of the mouths of honest English artizans by their devil's work of accursed machinery, replacing men's hands and brains.

"Not brains, my master," argued Madame mildly, "when the machinery is the creature and the tool of man's brains."

But the master had already retired into the farther end of his cottage, growling ominously of the horse-pond for man or woman who molested him with treacherous tricks of kindness.

A third hearer put her fingers in her ears.

"I was brought up in the south lands. I've seen the towers and halls where the good bishops stood and choked in the smoke rather than bring in the Pope to sit in scarlet, put his foot on our necks, and wade in our blood again. Good-mother's grandfeyther was a Puritan in the wars—could pray like a saint, as well as strike and stab like a man. She had his rusty blunderbuss, which was as good as a cast horse-shoe for luck, above her chumley. I be not your bargain, madam."

Here was an opening at last, which Grand'mère was quick to perceive, and radiant in seeking to profit by.

"My good woman, we do not love the Pope of Rome and the mass any more than you. We are Huguenots, who have abandoned our houses, our temples, our native country, for the truth. We have suffered like you. We have bought your protection, confidence, and friendship, by our sorrows and sufferings."

"I dunna know that we suffered," observed the descendant of the Fifth-monarchy-men, ungraciously and doggedly. "Good-mother always says her grandfeyther won his battles, as the truth is bound to win. And as to buying, I'll maintain you've bought nought from me, neither good nor bad. I'd traffic with none of your breed, whether Huggenies mean the brazen packmen with rings in their ears, under their curls, and French linen and brandy beneath the Irish linen and anise-seed water in their packs, and who bowed their knees, crooked their fingers, and kissed the broken cross at the Horse Troughs, where the four roads meet, before they were shot by the red-coats."

"Alas, my poor Jacques! The good God grant you saw beyond the symbol," murmured Grand'mère, the moisture dimming those clear, tender grey eyes of hers.

The speaker went on, rudely citing her unflattering examples :—

"Or the idle, dissolute dogs, players on the French horns, whom my lady brought down with her the last time to the castle, who jabbered their monkey-prayers to the pictures in the picture-gallery."

The woman was so irritated and alarmed, that she herself pronounced a spell to protect her from the offenders—a spell long current in Protestant England, and occasionally lugged out of dark, superstitious lurking-holes to this day:—

> "Matthew, Mark, Luke, and John,
> Bless the bed that I lie on."

This she sputtered, rather savagely than solemnly, in the tingling, perplexed ears of Grand'mère Dupuy, whose fathers had renounced prayers to the saints before the battle of Pavia.

Grand'mère was hard to be foiled, and was only braced to another essay by these outbursts. She had the exhaustless application, industry, and good-humour of her nation, and the devoted principles of her sect.

"We will try neither the old nor the young this time, my pigeon, but a girl like you—the girl Deborah Pott—whom I have caught staring in at our door and windows when she passes, and who once ran after me and restored my sack when I dropped it, nearly knocking me down as she did so. She is not pretty—she is an ugly, ungainly creature; but I think she has what is better than beauty, and only second to grace and goodness—wit, mother-wit they call it in England. But this lost child has no mother, only a stepmother, who gives her the kindness of the law—no more. Oh! well, it is good that she gives her that. She cannot make a mother's heart for a child who is not hers, and she may be so unfortunate as to forget to pray for it. Our Priscille tells me

Mother Pott is a poor widow with a large family to rear, and no wonder she is sharp in the tongue as steel or vinegar. Yet she shelters and feeds this Deborah with what help she can get from the girl's work in the fields, and without much hope of giving her away in marriage. However, Deborah has a wise woman's name, and if she has wit, we will give her a dowry—not that we have money—'silver and gold have we none,' my little Yolande, save what my son can spare to Philippine to keep the house and furnish the linen-presses and the wardrobes afresh; but we have our gifts and our accomplishments, though the country people here think so little of them. Deborah, with the wise woman's name, will be a doctoress. We will teach her our skill in the herbs, which our family have had since Bernarde Romilly stanched the wounds of the great Conde: that will be one dowry for her; and the cambric-darning, the lace-mending, the working of clocks into hose, will be another. She may not get a husband, for I have my suspicions that the English lads are not wise in their own interests; but it does not signify, my Deborah will be a mother in Sedge Pond, and she will nurse the generations of the future."

At first it seemed that Grand'mère Dupuy had finally hit the mark. Great uncouth Deborah Pott had not been so used to preferment that she should scout this; she had faced too many real evils in the bare cold lodging, which was hardly a home, to recoil from the strange Frenchwoman as the rest of the villagers did. Moreover, Deborah Pott was of an inquisitive, dauntless turn of mind, which disposed her to venture on the opening of any oyster which the world might present to her.

"My service, marm; I'd like to come and

try, if mother 'ud hear of it. She's wicious, mother is, when she's axed aught, because, as she says, she's worritted enough without that plague into the bargain; but she comes round most times after she's been wild a bit, and she's allers said she'd be main set up to be well rid of me."

This speech was delivered with many a bob of an original, irregular curtsey by the fluttered, important Deborah, whom Grand-'mère and Yolande had waylaid as she was returning from her field-work, with her long step, and short petticoat and shorter gown stained with clay, and her steeple-crowned hat, hardly browner than her brick-brown face, and her hoe over her shoulder.

But the bright prospect of success was soon dashed when Deborah came running over to Shottery Cottage, bellowing all the way like a lubberly boy.

"Here I be, to tell you—I be never to

come nigh hand you, or to speak to you again. Mother swears I be the pest of her life, and a tomboy of a lass that will stick to her like a burdock; but she'll claw me and whack me till there's never a rag of skin on my bones or a whole bone in my body, and she'll have the mischief shook out of me (and I be right sure it never comed there till you put it in, mistress); she'll never fee me to a wanton, play-acting, crazy old French quean, as would have her base job out of me, and mix me up in her vile plots, and leave me to hang by the neck at Tyburn till I were 'dead, dead, dead,' like Punch's Judy, when she were done with me. Lawk-a-daisy! lawk-a-daisy!"

Now Grand'mère knew the sum of the accusation against her, and for a moment felt cut to the heart. That she—a clever, provident, diligent woman in her day, proud of her house-keeping, and her various arts in keeping accounts, dispensing advice and assistance, rearing and training children, handmaids, and even apprentices and clerks, as she had done in the old velouterie, with which the Dupuys had been connected for generations, should be regarded as an unpractical, harebrained enthusiast, was most mortifying. That she, the humblest, most grateful woman in the world, should be branded as an interloper and a supplanter of other workers, a filcher of their gains, made her sigh deeply,—but that she, a Huguenot, traditionally descended from the Albigenses, with their Champs de Sang and Mas Calvi, educated in the most uncompromising antagonism to the Roman hierarchy and the Roman Catholic creed—that she, an exile for her faith, should be accused of vile purposes and plots, brought tears to her grey eyes.

To be thus confounded with her persecutors

and foes, in spite of her loud protest, to be ranked with them in their glaring errors by those who were very nearly as grovelling, degraded, and pagan as the lowest of the Catholics they condemned, was a bitter drop in poor Grand'mère's cup. That she, an aged widow woman, living in strict seclusion under her son's roof, and the adherent of a Reformer whose followers, in their reaction from license, profligacy, and infidelity, were staid even to moroseness, and rigid to austerity, should be picked out and pointed at as a light, cruel kidnapper and destroyer of young girls, was almost too much for her kindly nature. But still she was able to bear the grievous misconstruction without malice; which was needful, for Yolande burst out in a girl's vehement spite and scorn.

"But why do they abuse and slander us?" she urged, bitterly.

"But why?" echoed Grand'mère, meekly.

"I know not, unless they have forgotten, or never heard, how they admired aud applauded our first service in the crypt of Canterbury Cathedral, and only recognise us to taunt and deride us as we come out of the French chapel in Hog Lane, at the Seven Dials."

In the singleness of heart, which is akin to second sight, Grand'mère did more than forbear; she arrived at a partial comprehension of the cause of her failure. Her poor—her children as she had called them—had been too much children to her, as they are prone to be in those sloth and languor-inspiring southern provinces so long subjected to the yoke. Saxon vigour could never stoop to such fostering and to such helplessness; it were to strike at it root and branch to attempt this. Reformation, to be effectual, must work from within, not from without. The English, reformed by mandates of king and counsel, were not yet quite sensible of what true reformation was; while as to the French reformers, every one of them had had to go for himself into the desert, and had thus become noble, independent, and manly in his writhing agonies —protesting and steadfast in every nerve and maimed limb. And now the time was come for the two to meet and teach each other.

Grand'mère had been hasty, puffed up, and rash; she told herself all that, and it was true in a degree; but Grand'mère's faults were better than her neighbours' virtues, just as the doubts of Nicodemus and Martin Luther were better than the faith of other doctors of the Sanhedrim, and other monks.

CHAPTER III.

The Dupuy Household.

THE Dupuy household consisted of Monsieur and Madame Dupuy; Yolande, their only child; Grand'mère, Monsieur's mother; and Priscilla, or Priscille, or Prie, as the French tongues variously named a club-footed, taciturn, elderly English maid-servant attached to their service. The family was from Languedoc, which had been the very heart of the great heretical movement from the days of Richard of the Lion Heart. The people of that province have some of the liveliness of their Gascon neighbours, but it is crossed by Italian moodiness and passion.

The Dupuys had emigrated to England among the crowds from Languedoc, Angoumois, Brittany, Picardy, Alsace, Champagne, Auvergne, and Provence, where some of the hereditary nobility still bore on their shields the emblematic torches and stars of the Albigenses. They had been forced to escape with their lives owing to the long-continued consequences of the revocation of the edict of Nantes. They suffered under political disabilities; their church services, and even their marriages, were illegal. Their pains and penalties were innumerable, and scorn and contumely had been heaped upon them down even to the days of Jean Jacques, and the gushing, fermenting religion of nature.

So far as the Dupuys were concerned, the exodus had taken place twenty years ago, three or four years before Yolande was born. Silk manufacturers by hereditary trade, they had at first settled in the colony of Spitalfields. As years wore on, however, M. Dupuy, by his business qualifications, and notwithstanding difficulties, had attained a certain amount of prosperity and means; and as Madame's health showed symptoms of failing, he withdrew from greater interest in business than what was implied in his braving the dangers of the road, and the gentlemen of the road, in periodical coach journeys—quarterly, or more frequently, as necessity demanded—between London and Norwich. The family settled in the quiet village of Sedge Pond, which presented at first sight to tired, battered wayfarers like them as secure a place of rest and shelter as deceitful appearances could offer.

There the Dupuys had dwelt from spring to summer in complete isolation and seclusion, the sole interlude and incident in their lives being Monsieur's departures and returns, and the exciting risks by flood and field, from storms, overturns, and horse-pistols of which His Majesty's highway then presented a bountiful supply. But Grand'-mère was kept active by other impulses; for notwithstanding all her experience, she was unable to regard Christianity—even Reformed Christianity, with its half-healed wounds and rankling wrongs—as a religion requiring one to retire, like an Englishman, into one's castle, raising the drawbridge and letting fall the portcullis. She did not understand that to live in peace with all men was only to be attained by living apart from all men—"neither making nor meddling in their concerns." Therefore Grand'mère instinctively tried the innocent wiles of her own pleasant land; and from her sacred, sunny, hoary height of fourscore years she looked down full of hope, and was piteous only when the wiles failed.

The Dupuys, not merely exiles, but withdrawn even from their fellow-exiles, were thus thrown in upon themselves with the force of their national, sectarian peculiarities left intact; but they preserved their individual distinctions so well that they bore no great family likeness. The crisis, it is true, had worked powerfully on all the materials, but the materials were widely and permanently affected by sex, age, and personal history. The result was that they presented such warp and woof of good and evil as French Huguenots, English Puritans, and Scotch Covenanters supply each in turn to the dispassionate and candid observer. Monsieur was a Huguenot in name and politics, just as Praise-God Barebones was a Puritan or Erskine of Grange a Calvinist; he was on that account the more tenacious in retaining the little he had left to make up for the much he had lost. He was a zealous, energetic, influential member of that foreign society which has only within late years been broadly recognized as a moving-spring and leaven in English annals, and justly recorded as such. But even in those days it found some manly, generous defenders, and certain acts and clauses of acts were wisely and liberally passed in the British Parliament for its protection. But the defence was so ineffectual, and so weakly were the protective clauses put in force, that false prophets and revolutionists were taken as the exponents and representatives of the refugees, and to pay them back in fit coin they were caricatured and vilified even by William Hogarth, who was gentle to the Methodists. But there were more substantial outrages, too. Silk-mills, like that of Derby, were set on fire, and the sluices of great Yorkshire wears undermined. It was an ordinary occurrence for foreign workmen to be felled with bludgeons; and households such as the Dupuys, were like small colonies of ants in an empire of hornets.

Such a society had to fight hard for its existence, and had to be united by all ties whether kindred or selfish. The men who formed and cemented it, were certainly men of tact and vigour; and they have left proof of this in the great French names which figure in England's story in the succeeding generations.

But Monsieur Dupuy suffered the blight which the faith of many men, especially Frenchmen, who are far more speculative than emotional, suffers on the dissipation of early illusions and prejudices. Coming out of a concentrated, narrowing atmosphere, where the views of life were exaggerated and spasmodic, and having his eyes opened to the falseness of many of the lights seen through the highly coloured, distorted medium, and to the retaliating aggression and intolerance of some of the most cherished dogmas, he gave way to the reactionary feeling which has been ever only too plentiful among such a society. Monsieur was a good Huguenot in so far as he remained stanchly, consistently mindful of his own wrongs as a Frenchman, and was sternly opposed to the Roman Catholic Church. But he went no farther than this, and was in every other sense unmistakeably, undisguisedly, a man of the world. Madame, his wife, who thought differently, never ceased, openly and pointedly, to bemoan his declension, and to sit in judgment on it with mingled gloom and asperity; and though he was too much of a *bourgeois* gentleman and French husband to snap his fingers, he certainly did shrug his shoulders at her. Grand'mère, with her great, sweet charity, made allowance for his difficulties, temptations, and dangers, and bore with him, believed in him, and hoped in him. And the best thing in Monsieur was his conduct to his mother. He was a provoking, jibing husband, an indifferent, careless father, but he was Grand'mère's stay and support in all duty and honour; nay, he was more; the sallow, periwigged man of fifty was as deferential and as tender in his tone to the grandmother of the family as when she was the house-mistress, and he a chubby boy at her apron-string.

Madame Dupuy could not be called an unhappy woman, for she was one of those who luxuriate in their woes; but hers was not a nature calculated to make others happy. She was a woman of the closet, with the faults of the closet opposed to the sins of the world. She was sincere, constant, virtuous, and pious in her own way, but then that was quite a French way. She was more respectful and submissive to her mother-in-law as a daughter than she was to her husband as a wife ; while as a mother herself she exacted unqualified obedience, and was careful and anxious, but not fond. She had been upwards of twenty years in England, which had served her so far as a haven of refuge and an adopted country, but she had not discovered a single merit in it! She had been six months at Sedge Pond without crossing her door-step, except to attend the English church-service, the only service within her reach—the Lutheran form of which she not only deeply lamented over, but bitterly resented. She took no interest in anything in the wide world beyond her own family, her fellow-exiles, her church, and her country—the latter of which she had left to lying prophets and the destroyer. She discoursed continually on one or other of these subjects, dwelling particularly on the trials and persecutions of Huguenot history, until they seemed to shadow with a black pall all that grew and flourished, smiled and rejoiced, on the face of the earth, and until her talk was like a passionate protest against the government of the great God and Father of all, whom she feared, and only feared. When she spoke of her church and her country, she did not dwell as Grand'mère did on fruits ripened under the sharp frost of pain and anguish. She did not dilate with delight on gallant endurance, on love stronger than death, on patience, charity, purity, or heavenly-mindedness; she never credited or reported the remorse and ruth, the pity, the kindness, the generous pleading, in the formidable face of hostile despotism, of those who, like the Prince of Shechem, were more noble than all the house of their fathers. It was not of the Christian chivalry of Agrippa d'Aubigné in many a siege and battle-field, nor of the Christian loyalty of Madame de la

Force, that she waxed eloquent. Not of the noble, half-mad prophetess, Marie Villiers; not of the common ground on which a Bossuet might meet a Claude, or a Fénélon in his archiepiscopal chair a Paul Rabaud in the desert, did she speak. It was of men hung by the thumbs till the blood spurted from underneath their nails, of women frightened into fits by hideous spectacles, of drums beaten night and day to deprive the wretched of the last human resource—the oblivion of sleep; it was of desecrated temples and their dismal desolation, of the galleys, the hurdle, and the hangman, that she incessantly clamoured.

No wonder then that Yolande Dupuy, with her mental appetite fed on such a diet, should grow up sad, sombre, and scornful, with a perplexed, scared look in the midst of her youth and beauty. Had she been a lad, a young Hannibal, she might have been tempted to swear some deadly heathen oath that she would live to be avenged on the foes whom Christ tells us to forgive as we hope to be forgiven. Without Grand'mère, there is no saying how ungirl-like Yolande might have been. She would certainly have been more absorbed in the centuries-long injuries of her sect and race; more chilled by the dank, cold atmosphere of prisons and tombs; more unsusceptible to those sweet, balmy influences and bountiful consolations of God in nature and humanity, which call upon all men, however tried and however down-trodden, not simply to stifle their sobs and hide their wounds with the heroism of the ancient Stoic, but to take heart, look up and resume their march, in the confidence of free-born sons and daughters of the Lord Almighty, as knowing that their redemption draweth nigh. For Yolande had no relief derived from the robust, cheery presence of such a privileged, hearty, confidential family servant as a French Fifine or Solaire might have been. Priscille, though she had taken Yolande as a new-born child into her arms, and was inseparably identified and bound up with the family, was yet by temper, infirmity, and circumstance, graver, more reserved and taciturn, than any austere Huguenot born and bred. She was a gruff woman with a temper, whose humour was so dry that, like old wine, it required an old and disciplined palate to appreciate it; and indeed, it was true that old Grand'mère would nod and shake her neat, trim old sides at Priscille's brevity and unpremeditated strokes of sarcasm.

Grand'mère was the sole sunbeam in the family. She was a living disproval of any notion which might have existed that it was tribulation in itself which had rendered the family so still and severe. She had suffered more tribulation than any of them—than all of them put together—for she had lived nearer the darkest, most cruel days of blood and fire. Grand'mère had seen Huguenots, whose only crime had been attending a religious meeting of their own persuasion, walking behind a troop of infantry, collars of iron round their necks, and heavy chains linking them four to four and six to six, and yet daring to bare their brave heads, and sing one of Clement Marot's psalms:—

> "Jamais ne cesserai
> De magnifier le Seigneur."

Ay, her own elder brother, Blaise, had been one of the men who with cramped limbs, swollen by the weight of their fetters and the damp straw on which they had lain the previous night, dragged themselves along, singing triumphantly as they went on their way to wanton insult, wasting sickness, and an early deliverance by death. And not only this—Grand'mère's husband not being a Reformed pastor, who was allowed the favour of taking on himself without molestation the execution of his sentence of perpetual banishment—had been caught in the act of escaping from the country which condemned and abhorred him, and had to work as a slave, fastened to a bench, under the almost tropical sun of Marseilles, where he had been flogged and bastinadoed for three endless years. On obtaining his release, through a singular act of clemency, he returned to his home a bloodless skeleton, a harmless, light-brained, mazed man, paralysed not in body, but in heart.

Yet Grand'mère could laugh and sing now. It was not from French levity, but because, in her day, she could " cry with the best." These tremendous crosses and tortures had not been without their blessed light and their balm—not without their crushed fragrance of meekness, their lofty consciousness of rectitude, their solemn tender consolation of walking in the very footsteps of prophets, apostles, martyrs, and even of the great Master himself; else whence the force of the "Blessed are ye when all men shall revile you and persecute you?" But it is not so much in the actual endurance as in the after-thought of great tribulation that flesh and blood cry out, nature revolts, and all the smaller, meaner passions come out to coil and spring like a brood of snakes on their prey. To Grand'-mère these old sorrows were far away on the dim and distant horizon, divided from her by more than one life-time. Grand'mère was on those hills of Beulah near to the land where there is nothing to hurt or destroy in all God's holy mountain.

Thus the Huguenot household abode in the grey solid little Shottery Cottage with its square casements and hood-like porch. They were distinct and peculiar as any Jewish household, while the old village of Sedge Pond lay couchant in the attitude and temper of a sluttish, drowsy mastiff. Passers-by could see through the cottage casements ajar or wide open in summer, into the house; and through the glass-door or the wicket into the garden, which occupied a corner of the castle-park, with its terraces, its pleached arbour, and its grotesque monster or two in box or yew. But what most attracted the eye of the villagers was the pond, which they declared was kept for and stored with frogs, or the rapid growth of strange herbs and vegetables—chicory, endive, brilliant scarlet beans, which were regarded as being equally uncanny and unfamiliar. And then, too, figures were often to be seen moving among the flowers or seated in the rooms. Eyes were perhaps apathetic in peering at first, but there was no want of strength of disparagement in the owners when once they looked, and stared at Monsieur, more flabby than lean-fleshed, and not very remarkable in his rusty brown suit, plain cravat, knee-breeches, and square shoes with square buckles. Yet though he was more conformable in gait and garment to English fashions than his womenkind, he would seem odd enough to these stupid eyes as he led Grand'mère by the tips of the fingers to her seat at table, or from the pleached arbour to her room. Well was it that these villagers saw not all his graces of deportment, for he would stand many minutes at the back of her chair as courtly and insinuating as if he had been a prince and she a princess, he a young lover and she his mistress. Then the rest of the family made up a curious picture. Madame Dupuy, in the perpetual mourning which the later

Huguenot women assumed, sat precise and cheerless, with more wrinkles and furrows in her narrow forehead than contracted Grand'mère's broad fair one, and her grizzled hair as if in mourning, too, like the rest of her attire; while Yolande, in dress, was a facsimile of her grandmother, although the two models were so very different—the one so old, small, fair, sweet, and bright, the other so young, tall, and grey-toned in contradiction to the firmer, fuller outlines. There was indeed a flavour of tartness about the picture, and a permanent Rembrandtish gloom which was not without its mystery and its charm.

The public rooms of the cottage were not divided into better and worse parlours, as in other English cottages and middle class or small gentry's houses of the time, but into the man's room and the women's room. The man's room was half study, half business room, crowded and cumbered with heavy chests and boxes. A black cabinet, with numerous shallow drawers and doors quaintly carved with scenes from the life of King Solomon, stood in one corner, and escritoires, suggesting a lingering grasp of trade, and hinting of reverential preservation of family and party records and relics, in the other. The only visitors who had yet appeared at Sedge Pond were received by Monsieur before they were met and entertained by the general family, and that with a hospitality staid and subdued, but striking in its ungrudgingness, for it was the only outlay which the strangers, economical to penuriousness in English eyes, did not grudge and stint themselves in. The visitors were emigrants like themselves, more or less fresh from France, or worn into foreign grooves. There were agents of emigrants too, and with them occasionally came Englishmen, so.

allied to them in business as to have got over the salient points on which they and the emigrants stood aloof from each other. Sometimes, also, there would be a sprinkling of other foreigners—sputtering Swiss, bland Italians, and phlegmatic Dutch, as they passed to and from Norwich and London, in the interests of the newly-established or renovated silk manufactures which were carried on in small, dingy, and most inconvenient manufactories, where the looms, still waiting for Jacquard, were so complicated and so little adapted to the human shape and movements that the *canuts* of Lyons, who had worked at them for generations, were notoriously a crippled, dwarfed, and diseased class. After all, it was an odd shaping of circumstances which made a remote, thoroughly insular village, not even on any of the great roads, become a chosen meeting-place and rendezvous of those who, to nine-tenths of even enlightened Englishmen, figured, not without reason, as very suspicious characters.

The women's room had its elaborate, monotonous, time-consuming work—carpet work, embroidery, and fine lace-weaving, which Madame Dupuy did not disapprove of, but considered a necessary element of strict discipline, and praiseworthy in itself, however objectionable in its results. The room had no harpsichord, nor hint of diversion, nor suggestion of occupation beyond books of recipes and accounts. There were one or two treasured volumes of famous treatises and discourses by Reformed pastors, a work of Jean Calvin himself, and a volume for which, in its simplicity and purity, they had sacrificed, and well sacrificed, country and people, credit, comfort, outward peace. Grand'mère's passion for birds and flowers, and indeed all living things, was less artificially indulged than was common with her country-women, and this rendered the women's room barer, more rigidly matter of fact. Grand'mère's own room, in spite of its great linen bed and curtained doors, was perfectly simple, as became a Huguenot apartment, but she had her *jardinière* in the window, in which she grew spiked lavender and African marigolds, just like those the women of Languedoc stick in their black hair behind their ears; and she would catch herself calling to Yolande to shut the casement on a chill day, for fear of the cutting mistral. Yes, here, where the old woman who had suffered so much in the long past was to be met peculiarly, there were to be found grace, fancy, dignity, and a kind of refined bravery.

In the women's room the family, the members of which did not meet for breakfast, but supped their messes of soup stepping out of bed, or walking about the house, met for the noon dinner, which was composed largely of vegetables and such fruit as Sedge Pond yielded—a diet before which, as opposed to corned beef and stock-fish, it was quite true, as Grand'mère had boasted, that scurvy and leprosy disappeared. There they ate their equally temperate supper, not drinking anything so strong and substantial as home-brewed ale, or so spicy as elder-flower wine, but unutterably mawkish and insipid milks and waters of their own compounding, and, in rarer instances, when they had visitors, their vinegar wine. Monsieur pondered, wrote, and calculated, and waited on the mail twice a week, just as busily and assiduously as if he were still the head of a firm. And sometimes he would stroll alone on the terraces or about the country roads, or shoot small birds with a fowling-piece, causing a lively struggle in

Grand'mère's mind between regret for the fate of the birds and gratification at her son's diversion. The women worked everlastingly, keeping time to Madame's lamentations, or Grand'mère's praises and thanksgivings and sparkling range of observation and anecdote. There was no smoking, drinking, dicing, or card-playing; very little even of the feasting which then went on elsewhere throughout England among all classes, from ministers of state down to plough-boys. Indeed the prejudiced people of Sedge Pond esteemed this very sobriety as an important tittle of evidence against the offenders, and often discussed it in one or other of the great rooms of the ale-house as an unmistakable proof that the French family were guilty of far worse practices.

"A cannot and a wunnot drink like my neebours, because when ale's in wit's out, and a cannot afford to miss wit for my gunpowder plots;" so they would represent them as saying.

CHAPTER IV.

The Rector and his Household.

THE Dupuys had now lived six months in Sedge Pond, tolerated, but looked at askance, unmolested, but without having received a word of welcome as Protestant refugees. And yet there was, at the head of the church at Sedge Pond, a stout spiritual captain who with reason reckoned himself a good Christian and Protestant. Mr. Philip Rolle, the Rector of the parish, was one of the best and most influential of the clergy of his district. He was respected by all, a little perhaps because of his good birth, private fortune, and connection with the great Rolles of the

Castle, but still more because of the manliness, independence, sobriety, and morality of his life. And this was something at a time when the Church often scandalised the world by having in its ranks bishops, priests, and deacons who were ministers to iniquity in high places, and time-servers as loose and irregular in their lives as the grosser members of their congregations. Such things, when they did not excite violent antipathy, were regarded with indolent indifference. Indeed, the memory of good Bishop Ken and holy George Herbert, and the priests of whom they were the type, seemed to have died out.

Mr. Philip Rolle was a proud, opinionative leader, but at the same time a conscientious, active, benevolent magistrate and clergyman, a brave, resolute gentleman, and a generous man according to his light. He never missed preaching sermons like military orders, and read the service, whether well or ill, in winter's frost and summer's sultriness. He rode into the thick of mobs and quelled them, perhaps more by his undaunted aristocratic features than his ready riding-whip, which, it must be confessed, he was by no means slow to wield when any refractory sheep was straying from the flock. He would undoubtedly have refused to whistle the Word of God through a keyhole, as he denounced and stormed at simony; and his hands, humanly speaking, were clean, and his heart pure. But he was, notwithstanding all this, as fierce and fanatical as a Pharisee, without a Pharisee's hypocrisy. He would have objected to a dissenter and a democrat more than to an unbeliever and a tyrant, for the one he regarded as a masked, the other as an open enemy.

Thus the Rector had been vexed when

the Dupuys invaded his parish and accomplished a settlement in it. He was not ignorant, like many of his parishioners, of their claims on his consideration and hospitality as fellow-Protestants who had suffered in the cause of religious liberty. But he ignored them as long as possible, for he looked upon them as perilous neighbours and their views as dangerous stuff. He was without doubt a Protestant, firmly denying Roman Catholic supremacy, and boldly confessing and abjuring Roman Catholic corruption and error. Had he lived a little earlier, and had rectors gone to the Tower with bishops, he would without fail have gone to the Tower. But as it was, he had no regard for factious subjects, and his gorge rose at the French, whether Protestant or Papist. He classed the French refugees naturalised in England with the receivers of the royal bounty who paid it back in intrigue, conspiracy, and enthusiastic imposture. It was to no purpose, so far as Mr. Philip Rolle and vehement Englishmen like him were concerned, that the French churches in London and elsewhere denounced and repudiated such evil courses, and mourned that the actors in them were generally taken as the representatives of their sect and nation. The Rector was inclined to look on the Dupuys as more distasteful and troublesome parishioners than his old plagues, the meddling and levelling family of the Gages of the Mall, who were at least the spawn of an English brood, and whose vices and errors were those of England.

Mr. Philip Rolle, as was fitting in those republican times, kept a great deal of state, including a family chariot and a black servant. He had been rather lucky in his matrimonial venture, for Madame Rolle was a presentable woman, fair and fat. She believed in her Bible, her husband, her children, and "The County Chronicle." She was a good, common-place, shallow woman, who had known few cares or sorrows, and was entirely overshadowed by the superior intellect and will of her husband. True, she put forth her whole energy, such as it was, and laboured diligently in her small calling, in order that nothing should be wanting in her housewifery. Their family consisted of one son and two daughters. Captain Philip Rolle, at the date of our story, was in the army, and engaged in the American War. He was the very idol of his father's heart, and was reported to be a gallant officer and a promising young man. Madam Rolle, while she contrived that she should be the most notable woman in the parish, seemed also to have determined that her two grown-up daughters, Dorothy and Camilla, should never put their high-heeled feet to the ground, or soil the rosy tips of their fingers, which their mittens left exposed, save for their own special pleasure. This mode of upbringing was, of course, expected to render them all the better fitted for the certain, speedy, and high promotion to which their transcendent merits entitled them, and were sure to command for them. And since the Rector had a hand in the polemics of his day and a seat on the bench, he was too busy a man to think the question of women's education of so much consequence, that he should interfere with the training of his daughters. Reprobate parsons of the Lawrence Sterne stamp would interfere, and be very much set on their Lyds speaking French and dancing minuets, with the airs and graces of ma'mselles; but righteous parsons, like Mr. Philip Rolle, left the reading and the writing of their daughters, as well as the cooking and the working, to their mothers and to nature. He who was a lion abroad was, in this respect, a lamb at home. Thus Dorothy and Camilla had, perhaps, the best chance in England, if it were not frustrated, under Providence, by some sense and virtue in their own hearts, of being most selfish, uncultivated girls, full of affectations, extravagances, and passions, strong as in children.

The two girls, plump and cherry-cheeked, were puffed, powdered, and patched after the best mode, and lolled and yawned, with their lap-dogs on their knees, while black Jasper was actually employed to fan them in the hot weather. But when the wind or their humour changed they would walk about with their riding-skirts, used as walking-dresses, and the long trains drawn through the pocket-holes. And thus they would tramp through dust and mire to the next market-town or the next country-house, in search of adventure and diversion. They were not over-particular as to the kind; and sometimes they would succeed in coaxing their father to mount one or other on a chariot horse, while he would accompany them himself, seated erectly and stately on another, Black Jasper riding behind, with his knees drawn up to the crown of his head. For a whole dim October nay, or white February one, they would go about thus, spurring and clattering.

Mr. Philip Rolle was not one of those men who fight under women's colours. He did not even dream of using his ladies as helpmeets in his office, though the practice was ancient enough, and might have pleased a man who was conservative and opposed to novelties. In his own indulgent, courteous, autocratical way he was strong on the physical and mental inferiority of women, and their inevitable dependence upon man, and he enforced his notions by all sound laws, human and divine. One of the innovations which specially offended and disgusted him in the new doctrines which John Wesley and Fletcher of Madeley had given themselves over to spread, was that of women preaching and teaching, and taking it upon them to judge for themselves against the plain doctrines of revealed truth.

He did not employ Madam Rolle in parochial work beyond the superintendence of the making of a particular posset, or the placing the contents of her larder at his disposal for his respectable poor, whom he wished to feed and clothe by rule and measure, though yet with a certain faithfulness and liberality, for to the poor who had become so through their own deeds and deserts he was a stern gaoler and task-master. Dorothy and Camilla might perhaps languishingly or pertly distribute pence on days of doles or church festivals, but the Rector scorned female assistance of any more practical character. The idea of women, whom he acknowledged as rational beings called to love and good works, being employed in ministrations of education, enlightenment, or consolation in the best sense, would, in his idea, have been simply to strike at the very root of Protestantism. He would have mourned over it as a return to the ascetic sentimental sisterhoods of Roman Catholicism, with their famished humanity and their spurious pietism, or, at the best, as a drifting into the eccentric, unorthodox, lawless by-roads of Methodism. But Dorothy and Camilla were honest and modest, innocent in their ignorance and their respectfulness to their father, and their affection to their mother. They did not wholly want parts; at least they could not contribute to the evening cheerfulness by song, riddle, and game, and they knew the fashions sufficiently to spoil their complexions and injure their health a little by washes. What more could be expected of the frail things, since it was taken for granted that they also went to church when the weather was not too inclement, said their prayers, and resisted temptation in the shape of private acquaintance with profligate young Squire Thornhills, and such-like scandalous company?

The Rectory women had so little fault to find with their world and its morals, that it never entered into the light vapourish heads of Dorothy and Camilla that they were expected to be more than young ladies of breeding, of a little beauty and some accomplishments. Time, if it hung heavily on their hands, was to be got rid of as they could best contrive for their own content, and the maintenance of their very intermittent and wavering sprightliness, which, as was the fashion then, alternated with fits of lowness and spleen, when they would lie a-bed half days at a time, and fling their shoes at Black Jasper. But all this, of course, was done in subordination to the great aim of their own and their mother's lives, that in time they should make good matches. The sun of fortune had shone upon their horizon when their distant kinswoman and careless, capricious patroness, Lady Rolle, held racket at the Castle; and their fondest hope and wish now was to be invited to spend a season of frantic dissipation under her ladyship's game-bird wing up in town.

Nothing had more puzzled, astounded, and in a sort aggrieved Madam in the whole course of her sheltered, shallow life, than the disappointing experience she had had of her old schoolfellow and companion, Madam Gage, of the Mall. While yet a woman of youth, beauty, parts, birth, and fortune, this lady had risen up and resisted the imposing array of custom and authority, which she had been taught to hold in devoted esteem and veneration. She had declared that there was a higher law and a greater authority on her side, which she dared not gainsay or contradict, and which commanded her to come out of her family and circle, and follow her own course. Hardships, reproaches, mockery, contumely, and condemnation had not moved her. She had separated herself from her "world," and stood alone, and, what was worse, she had entered into alliance with men and women not of Madam Rolle's kind, and who were unlike her in thought, speech, and habit. Madam Gage had worn plain clothes, fed on homely food, risen up early, lain down late, and had established and maintained a household according to her own strange independent rules. Yea, she had even gone abroad, and laboured like an ordained priest, except that her labours were all among the poorest, most ignorant, and most depraved, till she had wedded Mr. Gage, of the Mall, one of the few persons of her rank infected with her craze. She had lived and worked with him, called all things by new names, and had founded every kind of unheard-of and uncalled-for institution. The husband and wife had stirred up the meanest working man and woman to try for themselves this new version of religion, and to work it out according to their circumstances and capacities,—above all, according to divine gifts profanely accorded to them. These senseless and audacious subversions of duty and harmony had been thorns in the flesh of Mr. Rolle, and had been carried on, to Madam Rolle's indignant marvel and dismay, under the Rector's very nose, and by individuals still in communion with his Church.

Yet Madam Gage, apart from her lamentable " perversion," did not fail in any of the relations of life, but was so true a daughter, so kind a sister, and so considerate and constant a friend and mistress, wife and mother, that her kindred forgot and forgave the disgrace and injury she had done them by her new profession. They restored her to their good graces, and reinstalled her in the place of the willing working member of the house, on whom, even though married, all troublesome obligations fall, and are cheerfully accepted, and patiently and faithfully fulfilled. And to the day of her death Madam Gage had never appeared to Madam Rolle with the bearing of a conscious offender, or even of a presuming woman. In her stuff gown, linen neckerchief, and muffling head-dress of frills and bands,

Madam Gage had looked the same grand, handsome, frank, high-spirited woman she had looked when she went, powdered as a marchioness, with brocade over her hoop and a pearl drop at her throat. If there was any change, it was a greater depth in her grey eyes, a sweeter curve in her full, firm lip, as though peace and rest had come out of the strife and toil she had chosen, and had lent serenity to her beauty.

CHAPTER V.

The Flag of Truce, and how it Fared.

"I WISH you to give me your company in paying a visit," said Mr. Philip Rolle to his wife and daughters, one day, as he entered the parlour with its Indian hangings, worked chair-covers, and dragon china. Madam, in a sacque, sat poring over her recipe-book, and Dorothy and Camilla sat with crossed hands and made faces in an opposite mirror.

"Where to, papa?" cried the girls in a breath, jumping up. "You must tell us, that we may know what to wear. Any kind of gadding is better than moping here."

"With all the pleasure in life, girls; we are delighted to go abroad with papa," put in Madam, carefully. "Is the chariot to be had out, sir?"

It is to be noted that Madam did not stand in awe of her husband. She loved him too well for what is generally understood by that phrase, and perfect love in this relation, as in every other, casteth out fear. She comprehended his character so well by long, fond poring over him, that she read what was in his mind as readily as a much cleverer woman would have read it, and she set herself to humour him. She was aware that, great man as he was, he was not superior to keeping his family in the dark till the last moment as to his intentions, and thus exercising them in blind obedience. And he now answered briefly, "No, there is no need for the chariot; the attendance of Black Jasper will suffice."

"Surely you might tell us more, papa," implored the girls, half whimpering. "We do not know whether we ought to put on our gauzes and mantles, or our modes and paduasoys."

"Either, my daughters; the question is not worth a wise woman's consideration. Granting that the wise woman's clothing was silk and purple, I dare avow she put it on at once and did not weigh it in the balance," asserted the provoking man, who yet hardly ever proposed to his daughters any higher questions.

Madam Rolle hastened to step in to still the little ferment and to dissipate the perplexity which was already causing pouts and taps of the heels on the floor. "I am certain my Dorothy and my Camilla will be charmed to have an opportunity of seeing company with their papa and me, whether they are to be in their mantles or their paduasoys. I daresay, my dear, we have to go no farther than the alehouse, to see some travellers who are baiting their horses there, or have broken down, or fear to go on and be benighted. Only, sir, if we are to offer them our hospitality, I hope you will acquaint me in time, as I cannot be provided with what I need any nearer than Redham. Surely my Lady Rolle and her sons cannot have come suddenly to the Castle without previous warning, or without the girls seeing the coach and the riders, when they have sat in the window there and diverted themselves counting every cart, waggon, and pack-horse that has passed this morning."

"No, Lady Rolle is not at the Castle, that I have heard of," her lord and master assured her, "and the object of the call is none so pleasant that I should be in haste to announce it. I think it is fit we should wait on these French cattle at Shottery Cottage."

"Where you think it right to go, my dear Philip, I am ready and willing to attend you; but, sir, do you think it equally safe for the girls?" hesitated Madam, for once in her life doubtful of Mr. Philip Rolle's complete discretion.

"Why, there is no fear these people will kidnap our idle lasses, and send them over the seas to convents to learn to be useful there, especially when their own women have preferred being put into penitentiaries."

"Never mind papa, girls; he has no real intention of depreciating his own, or exalting foreigners over true Britons."

"You are right there, Millie; but if we are to do the thing at all, we had better do it handsomely. These folk have a chit like ours, whom we may as well notice if we notice any of them; it is probable she is the most harmless of the lot."

"If you please, sir, we have seen her," said Dorothy, glibly; "a white-faced girl, who looks as if she had the vapours every day. She sails abroad in silks; and—what do you think?—carries porringers with her own hand, in company with a little old witch, who has always a red-headed stick—the same who threw Goody Gubbins into fits with her sorceries."

"Never mind, child, she'll not bewitch you when I am there to break the charm; and she'll proselytise long before she proselytises Goody Gubbins." Thus the Rector cut her short, objecting to petty gossip.

"I'm not affrighted," Camilla joined in, a little loftily. "And I wish above all things to hear the French prophets."

"What! do you wish to hear them prophesy, Millie?" argued her mother in amazement. "I hope, sir, they'll do nothing of the kind."

"I hope not," said Mr. Philip Rolle, quietly agreeing with his wife ; " but you need be under no apprehension, for if they do I shall instantly leave the house," he concluded, with an animation which sounded very much as if it would be rather a relief than otherwise to shake the dust from his feet against the strangers.

"I never stood and heard any offence of the sort," continued Madam, excited and flurried in her turn, "unless it was Lucy Gage once, when she came off her pillion and addressed the crowd which Lady Rolle was going to treat to a harvest supper. I was in the chariot, and Dapple had cast a shoe, and I was detained in spite of myself. I'd liefer have walked home barefoot. All I could do was to turn away my head and think to stop my ears when I saw a gentlewoman so eaten up with pride and false religion as to deliver a homily to rustics and gaping clowns in the open road before Sim Hart's, the farrier's. Yet I protest all I heard was no worse and no more untrue than that there was One who gave them all things; and that they should remember his great harvest gathered in by the angels, and should behave godly, righteously, and soberly at their feast. But even if they forgot Him, there was One who remembered them in pity, not in anger; who was ready to save them to the uttermost, and to pluck them like brands from the burning, even at the last moment, if they but willed Him to save them."

"Yes," said the Rector, " and the labourers went out of her sight and made themselves beastly drunk, and rioted, and put a torch to Farmer Clere's stackyard, excusing themselves on the ground that he was not a vessel of grace to be saved without works as they were; and all because a mad woman forgot humility and restraint, and wrested the Scriptures to her own and to her neighbours' destruction."

"Alake! Dolly, Millie, hear what your good father says, and take heed in time; for I knew Lucy Gage when she was as renowned for her modesty and sensibility as for her brave spirit and temper. And now that she is dead and gone, I doubt not, poor soul! she meant no harm; only she was led away and blinded and besotted by wild views, as her husband and her son are to this day."

The girls did not seem much impressed by this appeal, but stood with round eyes of expectation and curiosity.

"I know why our Millie wants so much to hear the French prophets," Dorothy said, putting herself forward to communicate information. "We had it from Mrs. Troutbeck, my lady's maid, when she was down at the Castle for the catgut to make the bell-ribands, that my lady bought their blessing, and won a hundred guineas at faro, and heard good news of Mr. Dick's ship within the month."

Mr. Philip Rolle frowned. He hated to speak evil of dignities, and he was conservative and aristocrat to the back-bone. He loved the very name of Rolle, as Dr. Johnson loved that of Beauclerc. He was not only a kinsman of the house, but he had been governor of my lady's sons, who were his juniors, in the old days before he succeeded to the living of Sedge Pond. He had sat at the Castle board on a different footing from that of most governors, having been an honoured friend of the clever, witty, and witless lady of the Castle. The honour of the family was thus doubly in his keeping, and was doubly dear to him, but he could not let the intimation pass without an expression of his disapprobation.

"My lady will have her folly," he said, dryly; "which doth not concern us much, save that we would prefer that it did not tamper with things sacred. When all is done, it seemeth to me that it should be the part of honest people, who hold that blood is thicker than water, not to prate of servants' idle stories, and trumpet the follies of their superiors."

Dorothy stood corrected like a naughty child, and, with all her womanly growth and fine-ladyism, put her finger into her mouth.

Again Madam interposed, and turned the conversation:

"Mr. Rolle, I am in a quandary about these French neighbours. I did learn French, along with drilling and the use of the globes, for a quarter or two at the Miss Cromwells' school at Huntingdon; but 'tis so long ago, that I am under an apprehension I have forgotten every word. Indeed, I shall not attempt to speak it, and I think I had better tell you beforehand, lest you, who are such a scholar yourself, should be disappointed and shamed with me."

"I shall not be disappointed, dame, and shamed I need not be, unless it be on my own account, since, though you are good enough to call me a scholar, and though the language was mightily affected at the Castle in my time, and I did then acquire some skill in it, I doubt me much whether I could pass muster after so great an interval, unless before such a connoisseur as you. But why distress ourselves with the supposed obligation, since we have a couple of daughters, new off the irons of polite accomplishment, ready to relieve us, and show off for us in all the languages under the sun."

"Papa, papa!" cried Dorothy, "how can you propose such a thing, when you know that last spring, when we rode into Redham, you forbade us to learn Italian because old Madame Viol had been an opera-dancer, and you said you did not affect the opera, and did not care for us picking up its jargon."

"And you took us away from Monsieur Delaine," chimed in Camilla, "just when we were getting into the fairy tales, and the contre-dances, because he sent Dolly such a set of ribands as she had longed for on her birthday, and instructed her to fib when you questioned her about it, and lied directly when you taxed him with it."

Thus Dorothy and Camilla declined the appointment, and vindicated their refusal.

"And suppose these Shottery Cottage gentry are also among the prophets, and begin to prophesy in their own language, it will be speaking in an unknown tongue to you," suggested the Rector.

The two girls looked blank at the self-evident proposition.

"Will my dear girls never be made sensible that their papa loves to joke with them?" remonstrated Madam.

"And softly, Mistress Dorothy and Mistress Camilla, I should as soon look to see Black Jasper do a turn of hard work for his diet and his livery, as to find misses of any kind prove that they had not picked their father's pockets by putting into the simplest practice the lessons on which he has spent a power of money."

The party started at last, and as they were complying with a professional duty and form of society, they were marshalled in order. His Reverence and Madam walked first, she quite stately in her parson's wife's hood and pattens, for the streets of the village were rarely passable even in dry weather, and he stalking gravely, in his cauliflower wig and black stockings. Dorothy and Camilla, having barely got over the grievance of not being allowed time to decide between their mantles and their paduasoys, went quarrelling all the way as to the right of each to a single extraordinary crimson parasol, such as Chinamen may be seen to carry now-a-days. It was a cast-off parasol of Lady Rolle's, the only one in these parts, and a great curiosity. Behind them again came Black Jasper, to whom and to his master it was a misfortune that he did every act of his life with exaggerated solemnity. He was a simple, timid, attached fellow, with a great gaping mouth, rolling eyes, and projecting ears which were like ebony handles to the ebony casket of his body in its green and yellow livery. His excessive solemnity and nervous fear of Mr. Philip Rolle were his chief faults. Why there should have been such an element of the ludicrous in the profound gravity and importance with which Black Jasper stepped with long strides while he carried Madam's Bible or her basket, or a cudgel for the presumed defence of the ladies, it would be difficult to say; but there it was, and Mr. Philip Rolle, a sensitive man, was keenly alive to it. But Black Jasper was an institution of the period, which could not be got rid of without barbarous injury to the poor fellow, who was so far from home, and so incapable of procuring his livelihood by his own exertions. Black Jaspers were fixtures and heirlooms then, and it was a lax and benevolent as well as a vain element in men, which made them adopt them. Besides, Black Jasper was Captain Philip's spoil, whom he had brought home after one of his campaigns, and it would have been a slight to the beloved phœnix of the house had the family turned the negro adrift. Mr. Philip Rolle aimed at being just to all men, and a connection with his son, however slight, was the greatest claim to his regard. But Black Jasper's inveterate, uncontrollable terror of his firm, sharp face, his clear ringing voice, and his abrupt authoritative manner, irked and provoked him. The negro, all the while, was like a docile, tender dog, and he but served his "Massa's Massa" the more sedulously because of his desperate dread.

The Dupuys were all at home, the women being together in their room. Monsieur was sent for to receive and meet the advances of the parish clergyman, and he at once obeyed the summons.

Never, perhaps, was there a worse assorted company, and Grand'mère alone of all its members was perfectly composed and at her ease. Indeed, at the beginning of the visit, she looked glad and gracious as well as grateful. But there was little wonder that Madame Dupuy, distrusting the English as she did, and bearing a grudge at all mankind, in her gloomy pre-occupations over Huguenot sufferings, should raise her neck out of the folds of her *fichu* like a bundle of saffron bones, and look down stiffly and sourly upon the visitors. And there was just as little wonder that Yolande, though yearning painfully after something like communion with companions such as herself, should draw shyly to her grandmother's side, and only look sadly and strangely at the giddy, tricked-out, affected figures of Dorothy and Camilla Rolle. They, on their part again, glanced contemptuously round the bare, sombre room, which every way contrasted with their ideas of French luxury and gaiety. But Monsieur, though bland as a Frenchman, showed no pleasure at the sight of his guests, nor gave any token of a wish to encourage and improve their acquaintance. He was scrupulously civil, he bowed low, and was more like a grand bourgeois, with his *noblesse des cloches*, than ever, but he did not grasp Mr. Philip Rolle's right hand of fellowship very cordially. On the contrary, there was a covert tone of sarcasm and offence in Monsieur's bearing, which the Rector was not slow to perceive and understand.

The conversation was conducted in fair English, so far as Monsieur and Grand'mère were concerned. Yolande was dumb. Madame Dupuy employed her broken English in making harsh, scornful replies which quite annihilated the simple phrases with which Madam Rolle thought to make conversation at all times and places. And not only this. To the still greater dismay and indignation of the Rector's lady, Madame was guilty of giving forth withering insinuations regarding the Rector's latitudinarianism, and so plain and direct were they, though in halting English, that even innocent Madam Rolle could not mistake them.

When the Rector, as a man of the world and a liberal Protestant clergyman, attempted to engage Monsieur in a discussion of French politics and the general prospects of Protestantism in Europe, Monsieur answered with smiling references to the exiled royal family, whom Mr. Rolle and his college of Oxford were supposed to favour without having risen and restored to them their kingdom. And then he went on to speak of the great gulf between Calvinists and Lutherans, which was so wide that the Romam Catholic bishops who had presided over the ceremony of bringing France to a unanimity of faith by the rough conversions of the dragonnades, had offered to overlook the mild profession of the last, so that the first damnable heresy were abjured.

"*Allons*, then, Monsieur the Rector," insisted Monsieur, with a wilful misconception, "one cannot tell whether to reckon the Protestants in Europe by thousands or millions, seeing that the Catholics bear no enmity to your pure form and simple hierarchy—your altars and saints'-days and lord bishops—that they regard you as brothers, in fact."

At the same time Madame Dupuy and Madam Rolle were at still greater cross-purposes, the one mortally offending and horrifying the other. Madam Rolle had begun by the simpering, unsuspicious inquiry how Madame Dupuy had liked the Rector's thesis on Sunday, and had proceeded to remark that her good man was acknowledged to be a fine scholar, though she should not say it. This she would take it upon her to say, however, that he practised what he preached, that there was not a better living clergyman, or a more virtuous gentleman in England, and she ought to know his private worth as well as another. Moreover, Madam had reason to believe that the Rector's theses had been noted and admired in high quarters, and that something would come of them, as something ought to come, for certainly they were too pious and eloquent to be wasted on an ordinary congregation like that of Sedge Pond. And did not Madame think that the music of the church would be much improved when the pipe and tabor were replaced by an organ such as Mr. Handel played on? Lady Rolle and others of the quality had generously consented to subscribe for it whenever they had time to get up the subscription and could spare the cash, and all they had now to do was to settle the dispute among themselves as to which of them should superintend the building of the instrument up in London.

In disposal of this prattle, Madame caused the hairs of Madam Rolle's head to stand on end by the unheard-of presumption and effrontery of the declaration that she did not like the theses at all. They might be very clever, ah! very clever, but she had not been accustomed to these theses, which might have been heathen discourses. She had abandoned her country, where the sun shone and one was warm sometimes, for the sake of the preaching which bade dying men flee to the shelter of the Cross. She did not comprehend exactly what Madam Rolle wished to say of her husband. As for the music of the church, she dared say the pipe and song of Sedge Pond might be very good music, she was no judge of music; but she had not listened with pleasure to the praises of God since she heard the sublime psalms of Bèze swelling through the hearts of a proscribed assembly, and awaking the echoes of the desert. Having overthrown and trampled upon Madam Rolle, Madame Dupuy crowned her enormities by intruding into the *tête-à-tête* of Monsieur and the Rector, frowning upon Monsieur without ceremony.

"*Oui, oui*, Monsieur, it is good to hear you on orthodoxy of creed and simplicity of worship, you who have ceased to condemn almost any deed short of fire and murder. From necessity, my dear Grand'mère? You are too good, too good, for a mocker like Monsieur your son. Bah! necessity is another word for greed, and greed is sleeve to sleeve with the god of a little country named Canaan, an adorable god which called itself Moloch. All the men are infidels now-a-days. They do not deny their faith, for why? They are too obstinate, too proud, that is all. Which of them would die for it? Which of them would count all things but loss for it? Count all things but loss! They trade upon it, they gain money by it, they adopt another country and another creed, they lament no more on the anniversary of the Revocation; they are consoled, they are rich as the world was when the flood came, as Sodom and Gomorrah were till the fire and brimstone fell."

The woman was stark, staring mad: could there be more unmistakable evidence than her loud railing at her lawful husband, who was taking snuff, imperturbably addressing her as "my very good Philippine," and imploring her, without *empressement*, not to agitate herself; while she faithfully and gently paid her duty to the individual whom Madam Rolle hesitatingly designated the "light-headed, aged woman, dressed up like Madam's young daughters," and all because the fine old Frenchwoman was a thousand times more elegant than the clumsy young English girls. It was far from safe company for them; Madam Rolle wished she were well free of it, for she could scarcely conceive that the French prophets could be more immoral, though they might be more blasphemous. And then Dorothy and Camilla were there, swallowing every word of the unseemly, scandalous defiance; though Madam herself allowed they were sometimes slow enough to imbibe what was good for them.

The joy of Grand'mère's hospitality was soon extinguished; but she commanded herself sufficiently to take part in the conversation, and do her best to cover the rudeness of her daughter-in-law, and the but half-concealed cynicism of her son, and to try, by her own sweet intelligence and bright vivacity, to make some return to the natives for their condescension, besides that of sullen recrimination and bitter pleasantry. And here Monsieur her son, and Madame her daughter-in-law, made room for her words, gave them respectful attention, with just the faintest qualm of Madame's self-righteousness, and the slightest hanging of Monsieur's worldly-wise, scheming head. It was the Rolles who regarded her as a second-rate, flighty character, and put no weight on her gentle interposition. Even the Rector, who had sufficient parts and taste to discern that the matter of her discourse was full of superior sense, and the manner of it more exquisite than that of any of the great ladies he had known and admired in his youth, failed to give Grand'mère her due, for sturdy English prejudice, which many regard as a grace, had blinded him. As for Madam Rolle, she was so stupid and stolid as to the qualities of the two women and their claims, that when Grand'mère, with tact and tenderness, introduced the topic of the American War, —in which all England was interested,—the Rolles deeply interested, since their son and brother was in the heat of it,—and ventured a warm-hearted, quite sincere reference to the young hero of Sedge Pond, who was then winning his laurels on the Susquehannah or the Potomac, and whom all the residents at Sedge Pond delighted to honour, Madam Rolle, with her one idea, made no softened response to breathing, feeling Grand'mère, but chose to make instead a final appeal to stony Madame Dupuy, asking her wistfully if she was the mother of a son as well as of a daughter. Then with a heightened colour Madam Rolle proceeded to the delicate investigation as to whether Madame had any countrymen engaged in the great war, for her Philip had mentioned that Frenchmen were fighting in the campaign; and though it was on the wrong side of the quarrel, the grounds of it were so far away, and they at Sedge Pond had so little to do with the mother country's right to tax a dish of tea in the colonies, that Madam had a dim impression that they two women might forget that their young men were enemies so long as they were not in personal conflict.

But Madame Dupuy knew nothing of the continent of America, and cared nothing for it, unless in respect to the Huguenot emigrants in the Carolinas. She did not even know that there was a mighty struggle going on across the Atlantic, by which men were being torn from their peaceful homes and were going the length of engaging savage Indians to come with their tomahawks and poisoned arrows to aid Christian and Saxon brothers against each other; and indeed England might have quarrelled with every one of her colonies, and driven them to the same position as the Americas, for anything Madame would have minded.

Grand'mère, in her rare good-will and her good breeding, was cast into the shade and thrust to the wall by the Rolles. Despair, however, was so foreign to Grand'mère, whatever she might aver to the contrary, in her vivid French phrases, that she thought better of the situation, and preferred to make the most of it, by addressing herself in the kindest manner to a humble neutral member of the party.

According to the etiquette of the day, Black Jasper had two ways of disposing of himself. He might repair to the servants' hall, or he might remain in attendance on his master and mistress. There happened to be no servants' hall at the Shottery Cottage, and in the kitchen Priscilla was as hard to make acquaintance with, and as fain to rebuff raw candidates for her favour, as were the heads of the house. Black Jasper had, therefore, after a full quarter of an hour of uncertainty and waddling between the door of the room and that of the kitchen, settled on the skirts of the gentry, taking his chance of his master's vehement impatience and scathing ridicule, and of the tricks and tyranny of the two young madams.

Grand'mère roused herself from her little depression at the sight of the sable face with its goggle eyes. She did not laugh openly or secretly, though she possessed naturally that merry heart which doeth good like medicine and is health to the bones. Grand'mère did not even need to restrain her guileless gaiety from considerate care for what might be Black Jasper's weakness on that point.

From the background Grand'mère waved

to Black Jasper, and he, glancing at his master the while, stumbled towards her. Grand'mère not only dealt with Black Jasper as flesh and blood, but she pitied him as the black child, oppressed, bought and sold, and yet toyed with by the civilized white man and women. She wanted to do what she could to make up to him. She asked anxiously whether her good *garçon* had health and strength in the cold north. She bestowed on him a small piece of money, with an apology for its smallness, and an entreaty that he would accept it for the sake of the ideal Negro, who was without doubt the type and pattern of many a generous, devoted black man. She opened her particular cupboard, and taking out some preserved fruit, recommended the sweet-toothed black to try it, and to tell her whether it resembled guavas or pines. And Black Jasper, totally unused to such delicate attentions, grinned, scraped, darted furtive glances at his master, and without waiting for an answer, obeyed his own instinct, and became on the spot a bond slave, for the second time in his life, to " the beauffle old Ma'am."

The Rector had spirit enough to resent what was little short of insult in his host's treatment, and more than enough temper to show his resentment.

"I perceive, sir, that I have been under a misapprehension in intruding on you," he said, in a white heat of wrath. "I may honestly say that I meant to do my duty and confer a benefit. My parishioners attach some consideration to the fact whether or not a stranger is known to their clergyman. But if I mistake not, and read your face aright, my absence would be better than my company, to use a country phrase; and you may depend upon it, I shall force my acquaintance on no man."

"*Après vous*, Monsieur the Rector," replied Monsieur, in his sardonic French politeness; "I beg to thank you for your intended protection. All I shall say is, that I think I can take care of my own head, and the heads of my family, my own self." And he bowed Mr. Rolle off.

Thus the interview was a total failure. Mr. Philip Rolle carried out his dignified presence haughtily, intending never again to waste it on traitors and impostors. The women of the Rolle family, for their part, were only conscious that the visit had been a mistake and a blunder, and, in a panic lest there should be more high words and violence, even though Mr. Rolle was a clergyman, they huddled together, and mother and daughters jostled each other out. Black Jasper, in the half-turned state of his head, was oblivious to all that had been passing, save his own delicious treat;

but the noise of the ladies' exit aroused him, and, throwing down Grand'mère's empty can, he started in pursuit of his owners, turning back so often, however, to make capering salutes to Grand'mère, that Mr. Philip Rolle observed the pantomime, and called out loudly that he would have his black rascal whipped if he did not behave like a rational creature—a line of conduct as impossible to Black Jasper under certain influences as sight is to the blind.

"*Voilà!* a good riddance," cried Madame. "Why should they come here prying upon us, and wasting our time? Yolande, child, to your lace. I shall finish the Genève account of Barbe Yot, who was imprisoned at Aigues Mortez, and clothed in a foul hospital dress, from which the dogs fled howling, and refreshed for further tortures by being plunged into the stagnant, slimy moat till her breath went out; and of her sister, Mesdélices, who was shipped among a hundred other young women in a transport, to lie like rats in the hold till they, or rather the ghostly skeletons of them, were landed, and put up by the government, in lots for the convenience of the cotton-planters of Guadaloupe and Martinique—that is what I could tell of their America and their Indies, but I would not tell it to these popinjays."

But Grand'mère sat and looked ruefully after the retreating company, the only disinterested company which had sought the Dupuys at the Shottery Cottage.

"I am afflicted that I have vexed you, my mother," said Monsieur, coming and bending coaxingly over the old woman's chair; "but it is true what Philippine says."

"Ah! for once, for once," interpolated Philippine, with great animation and asperity, as she curtseyed to Monsieur; "though she is not of this world, it is her pride and boast that she has not her part with the men of this world, like you, Monsieur, if you do not repent."

"They are spies and despots," continued Monsieur, quietly ignoring his wife. "They come to mock us—to patronize and meddle with us. Why should we let them come when we are sufficient for ourselves, and when we dwell in peace here?"

"I know not if you are right, my son," argued Grand'mère, meekly. "But for me, I cannot see why we should not accept their visit as from a good heart. Whether they *mean* it for good or not, I cannot tell. Where is the necessity or the advantage of living like owls," added Grand'mère, with her accustomed shrewdness, "when no one has offered to molest or persecute us for a long time? We are letting the child grow up more secluded and solitary than if she were behind the grating. I think we should have taken an act of friendship as if it were friendship, that therein also the saying of the Apostle to the Gentiles might have been fulfilled ; and whether our fellow-creatures mixed with us in simplicity or in guile, at least they mixed with us, and for that we should rejoice. Who knows whether our faith and love might not have changed the base metals of fraud and falseness on their part into the gold of true love? Alas! my son. But this, at least, I pray you to accord me, my wayworn, cumbered Herbert, do not poison the young girl's mind ; let her at least learn to hope that there may be some good in this poor old world."

So Grand'mère was left to talk with Yolande of the events of the day, to draw forth the girl's opinion, and resist and refute single-handed the evil force of example.

"I am sorry that you have not made friends with the English pastor's daughters, little one," says Grand'mère, shaking her head, in the wise clear prevision of wisdom.

"So am not I, Grand'mère," retorts the girl, with her latent repressed passion and scorn. "They are silly, these English girls, as well as saucy, Grand'mère, with such sauce—insipid hot water without strength or sweetness. Did you see how they whispered and tittered till they ran away?"

"No, I did not see, I could not see for sighing over a wet hen of a *malpropre, distrait* girl, who forgot to do the honours of her own household, and of her bread and salt."

Yolande winced, and endeavoured hastily to turn aside this thrust by a pleasantry.

"Grand'mère, I saw no bread and salt going, except with regard to the black miserable."

"Fie! you are miserable yourself, Yolande, to call him so," Grand'mère checked her favourite smartly; "and if you think silliness (if there is silliness, I have never said so) is a bar to friendship, you are no better than one of the foolish pedants of the Hôtel Rambouillet, whom Molière scourged. Silliness is a greater, more incurable misfortune than being a cripple, or deaf and dumb. Shall we not cherish the unfortunate? What mean we then by the terms, Maison de Dieu, Hôtel de Dieu, for our hospitals and our madhouses, but that he who giveth to the poor lendeth to the Lord. I tell you, Queen of Sheba silliness on the one side, and wisdom on the other, never prevented either friendship or love worth the having. It is only hardness and falseness of heart, godlessness and no love to spare from one's-self, that can dry and wither the heart, else why do I care for you, poppet, or, in reverse, why do you care for an out-of-date doting old woman?"

"Grand'mère! Grand'mère!"

"Grand'mère me no more. Some have said that silliness is an absolute requirement, that there cannot be royal condescension without a big and a little soul. But I don't say so; for it is blessed to receive also, only less blessed than to give. And you might have helped each other, you young girls," Grand'mère went on; "you might have bartered your best qualties, learned to understand truth and nobleness in other natures and under other names, and have grown more kind and tender, warmer at heart, and more glad of spirit. It is a bad friend of your age and station who is not better than no friend, my dear. I love not the religion of restriction—'Touch not, taste not, handle not, which things all perish in the using.' Is it not so, Yolandette?"

" Grand'mère!" exclaimed Yolande, coming out of a brown study, "why does all the world hate us Huguenots?"

"That goes without saying, and ought we to break our hearts for it? Ought we not to rejoice a little because of another sect which was everywhere spoken against once, and which happened to be the salt of the earth, nevertheless. In our case there are special causes. We were a great power at the first. Condé, Coligni, Castelnau, Mornay, Sully, Henry IV., all belonged to us. The Tremouilles, the Rochefoucaulds, the Rohans, were on our side. Catherine de' Medici and her women who knew best, made a fashion of singing our psalms. Then we were betrayed and betrayers, broken and crushed, and the vulgar loved to tread on our heads.

That is one explanation, and we could not help that; but we have ourselves to blame as well as the four seasons, when we cannot count our brethren's hatred all joy, and when it is necessary that we sing the penitential psalms for it. We have been godly, rigidly righteous, and enduring; but we have been at the same time haughty, stern, unmerciful, implacable in our judgments, at least when judgment was all our possibility. We have been like the elder brother of the prodigal son, my grandchild, who was very exemplary and very unkind. It is a marvel how many religious men are like him, considering who told his story, and pointed out how ungenerous and unmanly he was, and how unlike his father. But we had not all the good things of this life; thanks to God we were not like him there. We had hard lines—too hard for a girl like you to comprehend, *mignonne*. Consider, we were not allowed to call ourselves in law husbands and wives; our little children were taken from us, and given, with their share of our goods, to pretended converts, who were no better than traitors in our houses. We were forbidden to pray for his majesty the king, we were so vile; and when a poor pastor strewed rosemary on his young daughter's bier, and had her followed to the grave by young girls like herself and you, he was arrested by the authorities, condemned and punished for an impudent mimicry of the holy church's rites."

"And the English pastor, too, who knows better!" Yolande pursued her own disturbed indignant reflections.

"He knows better," Grand'mère repeated, emphatically; and then, to Yolande's bewilderment, the old woman finished unexpectedly, "I like that man. How he goes against the grain when he believes it is demanded of him. How he is honest and honourable! I could trust him with my life, could trust him better with my honour, better than all with my faith. He might detest me, but he would not wrong me by a straw; he would put his right hand into the flames first. He would sacrifice his Isaac, his Joseph, his gallant young Captain first! He is righteous; he has a will like that! He is like Jean Calvin in his will; he is not like Calvin in his burning heart and his keen wit; but he is like Calvin in his will."

Grand'mère, like all very womanly women, paid huge homage to manliness; and she, who was of the Church the earthly origin of which is said to have been "Geneva, Calvin, and persecution," comprehended Calvin.

"You speak of hatred, Yolande," descanted Grand'mère, in the enthusiasm which

Calvin's name always awoke in her; "Calvin was hated. It is not good for man or woman not to be hated, but they must be loved also, yes, loved as men's own souls, by few it may be,—ah well! sometimes the fewer the lovers the better. But Calvin was not loved by few, or a little; he was loved by Bèze, his wife—the poor widow, by his step-children, by Geneva, by France, by Scotland. People will speak of how he burned Servetus and clipped out a woman's hair. Go! They will not speak of how he held the hearts of a city, a nation, in his brave hand, and moulded them under God to religion and virtue. The great Englishman was thought to be wise when he said that the ill that men did lived after them, the good was often buried with their bones. When it is the very reverse, my child, then it will be heaven."

CHAPTER VI.

The Truce of God.

THE arrival and departure of the mail by the coaches which ran between London and Norwich, only failed in enthralling interest to those who, like the mass of the Sedge Pond people, received no letters, or only such few and far between ones as made great incidents in their lives. But even the Hodges and the Sams, the Jennies and the Nans, who got no letters, and looked for none, hung about, and never wearied of the chance of beholding the coach, with its escort armed and mounted, its guard with his sounding horn, and its sleepy or noisy passengers in nightcaps and cocked hats, who called for their dinner or for tankards of lamb's-wool ale, or glasses of French brandy.

Monsieur Dupuy was a regular attendant in the whitewashed porch of the alehouse on such occasions. He frequently received letters of outlandish shape, addressed in queer handwriting; and those who would unhesitatingly and adventurously strive to read them over his shoulder, would see no more than two or three lines of Monsieur's jargon, sometimes actually no more than a row of figures.

Mr. Philip Rolle was no less punctual in waiting for the coach's arrival, to get the last news of the war in which his son was engaged. When the news were very exciting, particularly when they contained any mention of Captain Philip, or when Captain Philip himself wrote or modestly alluded to his own promotion or any credit his company had gained, Mr. Philip Rolle would sit in state and read the letter, and talk it over in the porch of the alehouse, assiduously waited upon and looked up to by Master Swinfen, mine portly, consequential, self-seeking host, and his nimble, loose-tongued, cowed-in-vain partner. The great man would be supplied with a toast and a tankard, and a single pipe, for he would allow no more—neither to himself nor to any other person. As he sat in state and paid the lawing, he laid down the law and would answer all inquiries after the young Captain more patiently and affably than any one who had seen his high head elsewhere would have expected. Mr. Rolle would also wait on for the news-letters and prints, for he was much interested in what was taking place in London. He was always curious to know if Mr. Wilkes had committed any fresh offence, or Lord North's

Ministry had become better liked. But he would not discuss these questions on the alehouse bench, though he had little opportunity of discussing them in any other quarter, nor would he gossip of the floods or the robberies, which were common occurrences. He liked human statistics, like all clear-headed, active-minded men, but it was only the subject of Captain Philip which could unlock the flood-gates of Mr. Rolle's heart. Captain Philip's name, written in its core, was the one soft spot, to touch which would cause the stout spiritual soldier to unbend, and betray him into prattling like a woman or a child.

The Rector was thus standing one day with his ruffled hands behind his back, his shovel hat shading his eyes from the autumn sun and marking him out at once from the lusty labourers and the coach passengers in their cocked hats, as the last alighted to stretch their legs, examine the priming of their pistols, and swallow a morsel while the horses were being changed. Monsieur, for once, was not there. He was from home on one of his journeys to London or Norwich, but the usual knot of grooms, stable-boys, and tapsters were gathered round the body of the coach, as well as Master Swinfen and his spouse, with the working men and their wives and children, the Rector forming a nucleus. And the group was not bent on a passing diversion alone, but was all alive and expectant of a generous entertainment, eager for something to speak of over their broth cans and groat bowls for weeks to come.

The village was already lying under the long low beams of an October sun, which lighted with mellow lustre the "Waüste" bristling brown, and the Castle woods burning red and yellow in the fires of the first frosts. Important mails were expected from the seat of war. It was known that the rebels had invaded Canada, and it was fully credited that they greatly outnumbered the English army. Even though they did, however, it was confidently believed that they must have been beaten back with so signal a slaughter that the disaster at Bunker's Hill would have been clean outweighed by a sure prospect of the war's reaching a triumphant termination.

The Rector was drawing himself up, as one towering by anticipation in the reflected glory of his son. He was not flurried; Captain Philip had seen so much service in different parts of the world, and appeared to have borne so charmed a life through it all, that it seemed as if nothing so contemptible as the rusty sword or pistol of a ragged American volunteer could harm him. Neither was Mr. Rolle absorbed in his approaching exaltation, for he was privately instructing Master Swinfen to broach a cask of October, to have pipes laid out, and to make a dole of black and white puddings to the women. The order was overheard, and a whisper arose that the Rector had already received special intelligence, and that Captain Philip must have won a colonel's epaulettes at least. Indeed the populace would not have been much surprised although it had been a general's white feathers.

At last, with the usual strain and sway, and immense clatter and flourish, the "Royal Oak" appeared in sight, and was hailed with as much acclamation as if it had never been seen before. Way was made for it and its attendant horsemen to draw up before the alehouse door.

"Aught for me, Will Guard?" cried the Rector, breaking in on the landlord's usual inquiry as to what was doing on the road.

"Ay, ay, summut, your worship; you might set up a dispatch-box or a private messenger," grumbled the guard, presuming on the large, official-looking packet he was disengaging from the boot. "It is word from the Americas. We heard tell the *Fairweather* was in port, but we were off to catch the daylight before the town was up to their sort. You may just let us hear, sir, whether the rebels have laid down their arms. I have a brother's lad gone out with Howe."

"With all my heart, Will Guard, if the word is worth the hearing," replied the Rector, and, still standing in the porch, he broke open the seals of the packet. It contained, besides a number of papers, sundry small articles which the sender had taken the opportunity of forwarding securely—Captain Philip's old epaulettes, which he had worn with such honour, and had now put off for still higher distinction; a pouch in Indian work, and a little box corded and fastened—remembrances which the kind young Captain might have sent home to his mother and his sisters, or even to Black Jasper, who, coming along the street at that moment on one of Madam's commissions, sidled up to the others.

The Rector cast a rapid glance over the first lines of the letter, started, and put his hand to his breast, as though he had been shot, then stepped back and lifted up a grey ghastly face. Without uttering a syllable to the hushed, expectant company, the dullest face in which was awed and struck, he made direct for the Rectory gate, presided over by its stone monsters. As he walked on, the people, not daring to mingle themselves with his trouble as they had mingled with his triumph, looked after him with smothered sighs and groans, which at last swelled to a clamour of lamentation. As he went on, looking neither to left nor right, he stumbled over a stone in the road, and the negro lad, stunned rather than rightly apprised of the weight of the catastrophe—the great tragedy which had been enacted last fall over the seas, and after many a delay and detour had this day reached the quiet Sedge Pond home —rushed forward obsequiously to remove the obstacle from his master's path. Obeying an instinct, Mr. Philip Rolle was pushing the intruder out of his way, when another impulse seized him; he grasped the black servant's shoulder with a strength which caused Jasper to writhe and recoil, and communicated to the servant the misery which was wringing his heart and convulsing his brain, and which he must speak out or die.

"Black Jasper, Captain Philip's fellow, your 'massa' is dead, shot through the head last year when the rebels took Ticonderoga. They have sent me his epaulettes and his box as a token, I imagine. Do you hear, Black Jasper?" the Rector broke off, and went on repeating his terrible statement, with his voice rising at length to a shout, " My son Philip, my only son Philip, is dead! is dead!"

With that he broke down and burst into weeping, an awful sight to see—and so he entered at the Rectory gate, and walked through the clipped hollies and yews to the house, while the shocked and appalled villagers gazed and listened intently, and the touched travellers thought they could hear a wail and a cry coming faintly, but with piercing acuteness, from beyond the pleasance.

That same October noon Grand'mère had been sunning herself in the Shottery Cottage arbour, which was then hung round with tawny leaves and clusters of blue-black berries. She was looking at the trouts, still occasionally leaping in the pond which the villagers called the Stew, and at the bees also sunning themselves after they had laid up their competence of honey, and were resting, like her, with their work done for the season; and as she looked she listened to the robin, which, like a sweet and virtuous soul, only lifts up its song of trust and praise the more cheerily and patiently when the whole world languishes in decay and approaching death. In the autumn brightness of the home scene, Grand'mère's fancy was spirited away to her native land and the scenes of her youth. She was describing to Yolande, who was plaiting straw on a stool at her knee, how different from this England, now sodden in its greenness, was her Languedoc and Provence. She kindled up as she spoke of the glory of colour there was in the very salt lakes and marshes, in the arid limestone rocks, and the bare heaths of the south, contrasted with the green luxuriance of England, blanched by such dim light as fell from the cold, pallid northern skies. And she grew eloquent as she told that there were distant snowy peaks and blue defiles; and that, for patches of corn, meadow, and woodland, they in France had soft grey olive and deep green and golden mulberry and orange gardens; and that for honeysuckle and briony they at home had among the grass scarlet anemones with the living blue of salvias and the white of asphodel by the roadside, while there were tall pink gladioli in the glades, and spreading pink daphne on the uplands, and oleanders, jasmines, and bay-trees breaking the hedges. The nightingale sang there over April roses and November violets. It was such a land of fertility and barrenness, passion and repose, as King David ruled over, as the son of David walked in, saying, "Consider the lilies, how they grow."

Grand'mère was interrupted by Priscille, in her calamanco petticoat, linen jacket, and linen cap, advancing towards the pair. The maid had downcast, grudging, introverted eyes, not because she was a suspicious character, but because they had early had her club-foot perpetually suspended before them, while at the same time they had not cared to look at it; and she walked with a' heavy, dogged lameness, and carried a basting spoon in her hand, as one who minded her business, notwithstanding that she had an ancient quarrel with the world.

"Don't 'ee be overcome, old madam, don't 'ee," insisted Priscille.

"I am not overcome, Priscille," declared Grand'mère, sedately, though her peachy complexion waned a little waxen, and her grey eyes glanced up at her son's window. "What is there that I should be overcome?"

"Now, speak out, Prie," cried Yolande, jumping up like a squirrel, and scattering her straws to the four corners of the garden. "What is it? The good God be praised, it can be naught to Grand'mère. Oh, my heart! what is it, my woman?"

"Did 'ee ever hear such a child, did 'ee?" protested Priscille, indignantly. "She'll be mum for days, and then she'll break out chattering like a pie. An' she do have littered the garden for a week, and me with the beet-root and the carrots to lift at my own hand. If it isn that black beetle from the Rectory have come howling here. No, I don't call no names; but he is liker a beetle than aught else in creation, an' it be not an ape, and the term came to my tongue end.

It is all wrong at the parson's. News has come that the young Captain's gone—gone to his rest, madam, by a hard road. Parson is in a sad taking, for though he may have preached as often as there are hairs in his wig that 'all flesh is grass,' he cannot abide that his own grass should be cut down in its bloom any the more for that. The young mistresses are cowering and grucing like turkey pouts, or screeching hoarse like the bittern in the Waäste. Madam herself, she's lying a-top of her bed, where they laid her in a swound, and struggling to swallow down her mother heart, because she is still a mother, though she choke and die in the deed. The maids trow she will, the short-sighted woman. Now, madam, didn't 'ee promise not to be overcome?" cried Priscille reproachfully, as Grand'mère wrung her hands, and her tears—the transparent crystal tears of the aged—fell like rain, for she could still cry for others though she had long ceased to cry for herself.

"My good Priscille, let sorrow and sympathy have their way. Do not attempt to stifle the bitter spring like the poor Madam up at the Rectory, lest the soil be poisoned. Alas! and the sun is so warm even in England, and the world is so fair, and men and women are in such trouble, Priscille."

"What would you have, Madam? It were always so," argued Prie, dogmatically.

"No, big Prie," denied Grand'mère, recovering herself.

"And 'twill be always so," said Prie, still more obstinately.

"Least of all, my Prie," negatived Grand'mère, decidedly brightening up and clasping her hands in silent hope. "Have shame of yourself, a Christian woman, to say so."

"Leastways in your time and mine, Madam," maintained Prie, fighting for the last word, and illustrating it by a jerk of her club foot. "And since we have gotten our own stock, I do not see that we ought to take a burden of other folks. That there bullering jackdaw, Black Jasper, must see you, and you must go up to the Rectory, according to his story—a pretty story, when you have not been within a strange door, or bidden to it, since you came to Sedge Pond. If they forget me when they are glad, they need not mind me when they are sad, say I."

"Oh, that poor Priscille!" exclaimed Grand'mère, as if at a climax of vexation and disappointment. "Does she not know that that is the greatest compliment of all! A brother is born for adversity. See you that a Christian should recognise a brother through all disguises. And what care I, though they can manage their prosperity, to which they invite their distant relations and their slight acquaintances, without me. I— I love better to be the brother."

After all, it was Black Jasper, and not the Rolles, who sought Grand'mère. In the extremity, the black boy had gone so entirely out of himself, that he had acted on his own responsibility. His philosophy had been simple enough. Massa had told Black Jasper, Captain Philip's fellow, of his loss first of all. That had made the most profound impression, and Jasper was not without pride in his sorrow when he thought of it. Then followed the plain deduction that Captain Philip's fellow was bound to do something in order to respond to the trust Captain Philip's massa and his family had put in him in their distress. Black Jasper could not cudgel his brains; he could only leap to a conclusion. The Rolles had no near neighbours their equals in rank—none with whom he was very familiar. But a bright idea led him to except the French family at the Shottery Cottage,—though whether he had sufficient powers of comparison and association to class persons so different with himself, and incline to them as strangers also, is doubtful. But the beautiful old French lady had been good to Black Jasper, and he would go and ask her to be good to Massa Rolle and his household in their calamity, and to find something good for them which they might eat and drink, and so break their doleful fast.

Poor Black Jasper in his childish appetites was not so far behind the wisest sons of consolation. Grand'mère was disposed to adopt Black Jasper's view in part. She came from a country where guilds of charity and mercy have long established a right to the sick and the sorrowful, and take possession of them. The country people were good, but they were dull or gross. Grand'mère called them so without invidiousness. They might miss doing something which would soften the hard blow. These poor Rolles, she felt, were too much hurt to hear malice. Grand'mère reflected almost passionately, too, that they should have come to the Dupuys in their good days, and got nothing better from them than mockery and abuse. As to power to work her will, Grand'mère was the most independent lady in the land—she would never have dreamt of asking Monsieur her son's consent to her expedition even had he been at home, though she might have made an appeal to his humanity. As to being compelled to consult and come to one mind with Madame Dupuy, there was not even the necessity of asking her leave to carry Yolande along with her on her mission. The rule of the eldest was supreme at the Shottery Cottage; the patriarchal, or parental form of government dominated there, and power was vested in the senior, and was no more affected by her being an old woman than if the Salic law had been abrogated first of all in France.

"Quick, Yolande!" cried Grand'mère, "my capote and Madame Rougeole. But alas! the little red madame can do nothing here; on second thoughts, I think we will leave her behind; the colour might remind them of the poor young man's uniform or of his blood—broken hearts are so ingenious. Now do you comprehend, proud little one, what it would have been for you to have been friends with these poor girls who are brotherless?"

"I am very sorry, Grand'mère," said Yolande, penitently. "I do not think I should like other girls to come near me in my sorrow; but then, you know, I am shy, though not patient, as a Huguenot. I should have liked to have been able to help them now. These girls loved their brother, Grand'mère. I once heard them speaking of him when they passed us in our walk,— how brave and clever and grand he was, and what he would do for his sisters when he came back a general. I can guess how they hung upon him, and exulted in his uniform, and walked abroad with him in it, the last time he was at home."

"Tell them so, my dear; ask them to describe him; say you never had a brother, but would like to hear of theirs. They will vie with each other in showing what is their loss, and it will relieve their poor hearts."

The Rectory, which was usually the trimmest house in the parish, from its china closet to its kitchen-garden, already betrayed symptoms of that extraordinary distress in which the ordinary business of life is arrested and lost sight of. Nobody had any duties left them now that Captain Philip had been killed last year at Ticonderoga. The most sacred precincts of the house had become common ground, always with the reservation of the Rector's study, into which he had locked himself. The servants were wandering about everywhere, and doing nothing except contributing to render this day wholly unlike any other day even in its outward symbols of wretchedness. .

Grand'mère came, like an interested friend and house-mistress, with the face and voice of restored discipline. Her tact and discretion speedily and noiselessly removed the overwhelming traces of disaster and dismay, restoring order and harmony without provoking rebellion.

"The son of the house is dead, that is too true, but the clothes must be laid away from the wash, and the mastiff must have his meal. There will still be clothes to be worn, and you will not stint the dog for the man's loss—or gain. The beast howls, truly, and why? Because he hungers. You need not fear to do your work, my girls, *he* will not be forgotten: and if you wish to remember him particularly, you can still do it on the Day of the Dead, with the living not neglected by you. What! you have no Day of the Dead in England? Then you can remember him with the other blessed departed as you remember on your bed their Lord and yours, in whom they still live, and you can meditate on them in the night watches."

Poor Dorothy and Camilla, unfitted to cope with the grim giant Care, were quite unable to control themselves, left alone as they had been for the first time in their lives. But in their horror and desolation they were sensible that a friend had come to them, and they cast themselves with full hearts on her protection. Grand'mère roused Dorothy from the seat on which she sat shivering as with great cold, and listening, with fixed eyes and curdling blood, to a conclave of the elder servants. For sore sorrow, like sore sickness, breaks down artificial distinctions, and drives some men and women into the company of their fellows, as it drives others into the solitude of the wilderness.

And now each servant mysteriously and fanatically delivered her experience in the matter of corpse-candles, death-spills, death-watches, taking note of what she had observed lately, and comparing it with the result. Dorothy might have learned for all her life afterwards to look on death as a dark fate haunting her, hovering over her in her own person and in those of the friends she loved, and from which she could by no means escape, not even by prayer and fasting. She might have learned to look out for it in dim prognostications, to watch for it, and anticipate its cruel blows in incipient madness.

"Our Bibles say we know not the day nor the hour; but He knows—that is enough," said Grand'mère, rebuking the ancient heathen superstition; and she effectually shut the mouths of the seers, at least till Dorothy was out of earshot.

Grand'mère calmed and soothed Camilla, too, and overcame those wild hysterics which were shaking the poor girl's body like a reed in the wind.

But, in the depth of her pity and the height of her reverence, she hesitated to approach the chief sufferers, and almost drew back from them. Though she was acquainted with some passages in the works of the great English poet—in her day little known to French readers—it is not likely she had heard of Constance commanding the kings and princes to stand in her presence because of the supreme majesty of her woe. But she had a fine realization of the sentiment, and it was trembling on her lips, when she at last entered Madam's chamber.

Madam, as she lay there to recover and master herself, had just gasped out an odd wish, " I could desire that Lucy Gage were alive and could come here now. They say she was ever found in the house of mourning, and had acquired the art of drying up tears, that they might not drown the wit and flood the senses, I mean, alack-a-day! what will become of the Rector's sermon, and to-morrow is Sunday. Where are Dolly and Milly?—they are not affrighted of me still? Indeed, I must get up, good people, for my head doth swim no longer as if I were seized with the falling sickness. I shall have no need to be blooded; there was no call to bleed my boy when his head swam. Oh! Lord! Lord!—shot through the head!—I can see his wet clotted locks at this moment."

"Madam," said Grand'mère, "I am not come to comfort you—I dare not. I sit at your feet instead. I have had many afflictions; I am an aged widow now, ending my days in a country not my own. But I have never followed the bier of a dead man, and he my only son. Madam, how much the good Lord must have loved you and yours when He chastened you so much."

Madam looked up, but closed her eyes again with a low murmur, "Ah! I am a poor creature. Do not tell my husband, he has such heavy trouble, I shrink from such terrible love."

"More than you, Madam, all men of themselves beat their breasts and lie in the dust to escape it, but still He loves, as sure as the world moves. He does not love us because we love Him, either first or last."

"And can you believe He loved my Philip when He called him to his account in a moment without warning or preparation?" pled Madam, piteously. "He was good, my son," continued the quiet woman, growing vehement; "he had only a man's ability, and he had a man's falls, but he was honest, dutiful, religious to our knowledge. Still, what do we know? He was in camp in time of war, and we shall never hear if he was ready, and how he met his call."

"Again I say there is One who knows all that, my poor Madam—knows all the young man's faith in His word, all his seeking after Him, all his obedience to his father on earth, and to his commander here, and all the sharpness and suddenness of his mortal end. You trusted our Lord with his life; say, then, will you not trust Him with his death?"

"Then I will, for I must," submitted Madam, meekly; "but French or no French —forgive me for saying it—you are a good old soul to come and put it so to me. I wish Mr. Rolle could hear you."

"And teach me nobler truth, as an ordained servant of our Master,—is it not so?" asked Grand'mère. "Ah! Madam, when we have crossed the river and thrown off our rags for His raiment, shall we stop and ask each other whether we are French or English, or—(you shudder, but you can say it, good woman)—American? No, nor even whether we are Protestant or Catholic; but only whether we bear the name of the Cross-bearer who bore our sorrows as well as our sins."

"Mother—yes, I hope you will let me

pay you the duty and service I owe you to call you so, for I remember they all called you mother, or grandmother, that day in summer, long ago, when we spoke of him, and I was deceived and believed myself a rich mother still; and he was mouldering under the damp leaves of those great forests he used to tell us of (for he served before in Canada, against your people: you will not mind it now, you are too sorry for us, and too kind);—he was so clever, almost as clever as his father, and the gallantest soldier in the British army; he twice had the thanks of his regiment presented to him, it was writ to his father. He saved a fort from being surprised in the East Indies, and nobody could save him,—but I do not blame his comrades; he would not have blamed them, for he loved them as brothers. I am a simple parson's wife, but I thank God I can remember all that. You are old enough to be my mother—no offence, madam—and I shall not forget your coming to us in our sorrow. What although you— no, not you, but your family—all but shut the door in our faces when we went to see you? I daresay you mistook us, or had some reason for your ill-behaviour. I declare you have done a great deal better than show us the most finished politeness. I shall tell Mr. Rolle when he is able to hear it; and he will thank you, and his thanks are worth the having. I shall tell Lady Rolle, our patroness, when she comes down to the Castle, and she may do something for your Spitalfields colony. Now, I am on no ceremony with you, I am going to dismiss you, for I must rise and go to Philip's father."

"But he will not receive you," said the Rector, as he walked into his wife's room, " for Philip's father comes to Philip's mother, because the woman is the weaker vessel, and it is for the man to honour and cherish her —that is how I read the text, Madame Dupuy."

He was white and shaken, a man who had aged ten years in a day. He was a little fallen in the face yet when he tried to smile, but his suit was in decent order— possibly his head had been anointed, and his face washed also, and all his resolution and manliness given back to him. He had wrestled for that as well as for resignation, and his Master was no niggard; he had got all he sought.

"No," corrected Madam, "you name the younger, bitter woman; but I do not think anybody will be bitter to us again. Philip— ah me! the only Philip I have left!—this is the old dame whom everybody called Grand'mère."

"I do not remember; I believe my memory as well as my faith faileth me.

Don't contradict me, Millie; the woman's place is to be silent and listen to the man. I think even this old French madame—Madame Dupuy, mère, be it—will not dispute that quite, in precept, whatever she may do in example. I rated my dear son's promotion too low, and that is why my faith failed me, and so I bore a false testimony before my people. I was too low myself, and too worldly-minded, though I am a priest. French priests err in that way too sometimes, do they not, madame? My boy has his promotion, the very highest. He died at his post, and I shall stand at mine. I pray God that He may give me strength to stand at his altar to-morrow, and bear a true testimony in returning thanks for Philip's heavenly promotion. I would have celebrated his earthly rise in the ale-house, but only God's house is fit when the step is to the skies."

"Monsieur," cried Grand'mère, forgetting her English, and her avoidance of all sectarian allusion at the same time, "you speak nobly, you speak like Jean Calvin himself."

"Ha!" exclaimed Mr. Philip Rolle, with a faint gleam of gratification, "you are too good, you do me too much honour. I do not hold Calvin's tenets, but I respect the man. He was no anarchist, no latitudinarian."

Thus it happened that in the days of bruised and broken hearts there was a truce in the national and sectarian hostilities. A compromise was effected, from which Monsieur and Madame Dupuy simply stood aloof; but Grand'mère was no longer a stranger to the Rolles, Yolande went to the Rectory, and was courteously and kindly received by the Rector and his wife; Dorothy and Camilla came to the Shottery Cottage, and were tolerated by Monsieur and Madame

—borne with, indulged, and indirectly taught by Grand'mère.

About the same time that the news came of the gallant young Captain Philip Rolle's death in a land-fight, there arrived also word of the death of one of Lady Rolle's younger sons, a naval officer, in a sea-fight, in which the renegade Paul Jones had a hand. But, though Sedge Pond had a little pride in having contributed two heroes and martyrs to English history, stirred thereto by the Roman spirit of Mr. Philip Rolle, who would fain have felt himself, and called on others to feel, a stern joy in the noble sacrifice, all that Sedge Pond heard or saw of the Rolle of the Castle's death was the messenger who hurried down to hang up the hatchment on the wall.

CHAPTER VII.

Squire Gage, who Rode and Read—The Young Squire who walked by his Father's Bridle—The Ministry of Women.

VISITS, like misfortunes, come not singly. The Dupuys, who had been six months at Sedge Pond without having been waited on by a neighbour, were within a month after the Rector's demonstration required to throw open their doors to a couple of country gentlemen, who had travelled half a day's journey out of their direct road to call upon the French family. They appeared in a guise so strange as to puzzle and confound even

Grand'mère's eyes, accustomed though they were to many of the strange sights of that strange time.

"Here be a Bedlamite and his keeper," said Priscille, announcing the strangers. "They have got in at the garden-door, and comed up the path, and now they be a-pounding at the house-door."

The family were thus called in considerable tremor to the lattice-windows. Happily Monsieur was at home this time, and the moment he looked out he dissipated all fears.

"*Oh! ça*, they are harmless. I know them. They are enthusiasts, like some of our own people, and spoken against everywhere, too. You will like to know them, mother; and though you were to offend them to-morrow, and even sin against their fine laws, as so many Englishmen themselves do, they are so enamoured of peace, these brave people, that they would not cite you to their courts of justice."

Monsieur had been either misinformed or had made a mistake between the Quakers and the Methodists.

"Let them come in, Priscille," he continued.

The chief peculiarities of dress and gait which had struck the Dupuy household were in the elder man. He was stout and middle-aged, with a capacious forehead and violet eyes, in which there was a wonderful mixture of observation and meditation. He had a good composite English nose, a full, flexible mouth, and a double chin, which was yet nowise gross. He wore his own black hair, which hung down on each side of his face till it reached his collarless coat and his cravat, and was abundantly sprinkled with grey, but without any trace of powder. He had on a broad-brimmed hat, like a parson's, but the rest of his dress did not correspond, being of homely, well-worn velveteen—coat, vest, and breeches, the latter with leathern gaiters. There was not one item of adornment in his costume, neither lace nor braid, shoe-buckle nor cravat-brooch, yet it was unmistakably the costume of a gentleman. Nay, the "grand simple" in style, after which some of the finest gentlemen of the day had the taste to hanker, did something to bring out the unconscious manly dignity of a figure which was in itself heavy and clumsy; and the perpetual pondering on the highest themes had taken away from the expression of the beautiful eyes what might have been the egotism and coarse rusticity of a self-taught country squire.

The strange gentleman had ridden a grey cob as stout, middle-aged, and apparently as studiously-inclined as himself. As he had ridden, he had read in a large book, with brown calf binding, which lay open across his horse's neck, and ambling along sedately, he had come upon an interesting passage just as he had reached the gate. Priscille's wonderment and scorn had been roused by his sitting stock-still like a statue for a few minutes to finish it before alighting, apparently with the consent of his beast, too, while his companion fastened the horse-bridle in the ring at the garden-door.

The younger man was common-looking in comparison, though he was a comely lad, perhaps a little over twenty, and big and broad-shouldered for his age. One could have seen that he was the old man's son, though he appeared so different, for he had his father's nose, mouth, and chin, along with a square, compact forehead of his own, and eyes inclining more to the steady blue than the changing violet. He was in the dress of his years and station: buckskin breeches, riding-boots, a red vest, and large shining buttons on his coat, while his hat had one of the numerous cocks which in turn was given to that important piece of apparel. But though the younger had all the advantage of dress which the elder wanted—though he had youth and the grace of youth on his side, he nevertheless failed in the special traits which marked the other. His face indicated breeding, fair parts, spirit, sense, modesty, kindliness, and was indeed a singularly fresh, honest, and healthful young face, among the many faces then prematurely wasted and polluted with the hot flush of passion and vice. It was a face, too, in which goodliness seemed to be progressive, like the slow growth of many a bounteous, fruitful tree; but one which, on account of this very slowness, would the more readily recommend itself to English hearts. Still, it was without either the dazzling gleam and glory of genius, or suggestions of individual and searching experiences, such as excited the curiosity and commanded the interest of every one who looked upon the elder man.

The father and son were journeying together in such cordial good-fellowship as many a parent and child might have envied, though the one was on horseback and the other on foot, and the one studying in unpropitious circumstances a volume of which the other did not care to construe a line now that his school tasks were finished. That other was studying the clouds, the flights of birds, the effects of soils in their growth, the rearing of colts and heifers; and he had not merely a quick eye to what was notable and picturesque in these details, for he had inherited that side of his father's temperament, but had also along with it a practical knowledge, love, and assiduity such as Squire Gage of the Mall, with all his wit, book-lore, and earnestness, had never pretended to.

As Squire Gage passed under the roof of the Shottery Cottage, he raised his hat, and said, so low and solemnly that it seemed a movement of the man's soul, and not a form of words from his lips: " Peace be to this house !" while his companion took off his hat and bowed his head reverently.

"You are welcome, gentlemen," said Monsieur, with his natural urbanity, as he came forward, while the women made their curtseys; "you are welcome the more that I cannot for my life tell to what I am to attribute the honour of this visit."

"You are to take it, and our most hearty service, sir," announced Squire Gage, in a deep-toned, full, melodious voice, such as with the early Methodist leaders was a direct personal qualification for their work; "they form a very small acknowledgment of the great debt we owe to a dear friend of ours, and a countryman of yours, who fell asleep too early for his parish, his circuit, England, and Christendom,—Fletcher of Madeley. I would fain hope I may hit on some precious memorial of my brother's early friends and his first youth among his Protestant countrymen."

Monsieur taxed his memory in vain. Even Grand'mère could not recall such a one among all the Fléchiers she had known or heard of, even although one of them had been a famous orator, a Fléchier who was a soldier in his youth, had quitted the army, studied for the Church, emigrated to England, and settled there, and had come forward in the van of the beleaguering host of the Methodists, the beloved friend of its choicest spirits, the truest gentleman and most faithful servant of his Master England had ever received into her Church's ranks.

But it did Squire Gage good even to speak of Fletcher of Madeley, and of those rough but brave days when he had known well-born gentlemen, famous scholars, impassioned, meek Christians, lodging in outhouses and barns, without fire or candle, when they trudged along the dangerous roads with their saddle-bags strapped on their backs, brushed each other's shoes and washed each other's potatoes, preached forty hours in a week, and prayed in every house they entered, from five of the clock in the bitter winter mornings till past midnight. Ay, he remembered those days, and loved to think of them too, when they were set upon by bull-dogs, pelted with paving-stones, and drummed out of towns by the public drummer. It did Squire Gage good to speak of the gallant campaign in which he had borne his part, and it warmed his heart to hear the French tongues and to see the French faces. So Fletcher of Madeley had spoken and felt, when he struggled with his consumptive cough to address his people for the last time; so he had looked when he took off his hat to his pew-opener; and when he plucked the cushion from his pony-chaise and presented it that the fractured limb of the savage yeoman, who had been his greatest enemy, migh rest upon it.

There was a freemasonry between the old Methodist and the old Huguenots, though they differed in many important particulars.

Squire Gage spoke of the rise of Methodism, eagerly but simply. The deeds done had been devoted, gentle, generous deeds, yet there had been nothing wonderful in them save the grace of God vouchsafed by his Son, and reflected faintly in the lives of men whose faces, when they were looked upon by the sympathetic eyes of their generation, seemed as though they had been the faces of angels. Such men were the two great brothers, Mr. John and Mr. Charles Wesley, Fletcher, and Whitfield. For all that, the last Squire Gage had opposed Whitfield, and taken his stand on the Arminian side of the famous controversy. But our Suire had learnt the broadest of charity from a broad experience. He had dealt with publicans and sinners of the first water, with Sadducees of all grades, from the heartless negatives of Lord Chesterfield, delivered in Louis Quinze French, and interrupted by incomparable liftings of his hat and takings of snuff, down to the bullying, blustering, blaspheming rodomontade of some Billy Blue, broken in upon by fierce squirts of tobacco-juice and defiant hitches of his trowsers' belt. He had encountered Pharisees of every rank and shade, from those whose gain was a bishop's mitre down to squalid, railing men, whose temptation was the miserable three-pounds-a-quarter pittance of the travelling Methodist preacher. He had known, too, Israelites without guile, whose mark had to stand for a signature; and Israelites who burnt their Platos and Livys lest their books should tempt them into intellectual pride, or withdraw them from the narrow way in which alone they could walk, and save their own and their fellow-creatures' souls. And Squire Gage was not like Ignatius Loyola, who vowed himself to the Virgin, and banished women from the roll of his order; for he had known Maries who had washed and mended their rags in order that they might do all things decently; or had laid aside their brocades and pearl drops, and appeared for ever afterwards in homely calimanco and muslin. He had known some who had set their diamonds in the unplastered walls of primitive chapels, who had given up their cards for hymn-books, and announced their auctions that they might provide houses of refuge for the poverty-stricken, the sick, and the sinful. Squire Gage had made many such friends in the dens of great cities, in the wilds of America, on shipboard, and at Moorfields.

The Squire's nature was so liberal, generous, and finely attuned to sympathy, that he made little of his own claims and much of his neighbours', and so he addressed the Dupuys with a deferential wave of the hand and a manly apology for taking up the time of the interview. "I am advised not to detain you further with my poor personal narratives; an elderly man waxes both heavy and garrulous, and therefore Mr. John warned his preachers not to suffer the devil to tempt them into long sermons. But may I beg the favour of a few fresh particulars of your honourable history? Indeed, I am credibly informed that you have been most blessed martyrs."

"Yes, indeed, martyrs *par-ci* and martyrs *par-là*; but I leave the question of the martyrs," declared Monsieur, indifferently. "I say we have been honest men stripped of our rights and privileges, and brutally pillaged and outraged, and that if we pay our enemies back in their own money, they have worked for their wages,—that is all."

"That is to leave the question of the martyrs, sure enough," answered Squire Gage, gravely; "for martyrs, and for that matter, brave, true patriots, do not avenge themselves. My dear sir, I pray you think better of it."

"Ta, ta, ta, my dear Monsieur Gage; it is my own business."

"I deny that," asserted the Squire, eagerly; "I deny that any man's business is his own if it be likely to injure or ruin him, and if it is granted that he is one of many brethren."

"Say it to him, Monsieur," adjured Madame Dupuy, "when the cats run on the roof the mice dance on the planks. Ah well! yes, the famine drives the wolves out of the forest. My husband will ask permission to blow his nose on the one hand, and he will persist in following his worldly, reckless courses on the other. All men are Demases in these degenerate days."

"Madam!" responded Squire Gage, turning round in mild astonishment and deprecation upon the narrow, dark face, with the rage of the contest for ever burning fiercely in it; and, true to his Methodist principles, he rebuked the error. "I also am a man, and I have yet to learn that these days in which we live are degenerate pays. I fancy they are a mighty deal better than those in which Mary burnt the bishops, or Elizabeth fined the Puritans, or Anne thought of bringing back the Pope and the Pretender, or your Charles and Catherine massacred your fathers, or your Louis sold them as slaves; only I conclude there has been some good in all events and at all times, else God would not have suffered them, any more than the world. Moreover, I have read, both in the law and the Gospel, that the man is the head of his house; therefore, even although the head were as far wrong as you say, I see not that the tail would have any call to rise up and lash its own natural sovereign."

"But they tell me that your sect allows the public ministry of women?" questioned

Grand'mère, partly to provide for the subsiding of any offence which might have arisen from the plain speaking of Mr. Gage. Such plain speaking was but small offence to her, when there was nothing in it of the "stand aside, I am holier than thou." At the same time, Grand'mère had a vehement prejudice against the public ministry of women. Like other Frenchwomen whose social influence was immense, she was inclined to hold in aversion every independent influence exerted by women.

"Yes, my dear old dame," confirmed the Squire, bending gladly to the benign foreign face which was least strange to him, since it reminded him most of the face of Fletcher of Madeley; "and we are minded to say, though it is not a gallant saying, that if an ass rebuked Balaam, and a cock rebuked Peter, surely a woman may rebuke sin."

"Certes! that is not putting the similes too high," acknowledged Grand'mère, with her silvery laugh; "still, you see, I have heard of a certain epistle called Corinthians, and in the epistle premier there is a certain chapter numero xiv., verses 34 and 35, where we read something on the preaching and the teaching of women; now, what of that, sir?"

"We opine, madam, that the verses refer to church government and discipline, and we ordain not, nor do our women presume that they should settle the disputes in our conferences, or control the management of our circuits. But to what purpose have you women your tender logic of the heart, compared with which ours is so tough and dry? For the use of your husbands and children only? Why, that is selfish at the best. And what if your husbands and children do not want it? What if you have neither husbands nor children? You will confess that Deborah, and not Lapidoth, judged Israel, and Anna spoke of the child to all who looked for his coming. That was before the days of the great Apostle Paul, I grant you; but methinks he would not have shut the mouths of those women. When I was so happy, and my dame so much less happy than she is now, in that she still abode with me, I used to find that when I spoke to a crowd of fellow-sinners, more by token when they were poor, work-worn, dull, or distraught men and women, and I was apt to fly far over their heads, my good woman never came after me but she went straight to their hearts. Ah! I wish you could have heard her. If you had done so, you would never have controverted women speaking in the cause of their Lord again. She had Chrysostom's golden mouth, and could lull and disarm the most raging opposition of the natural man, could overcome the most tormenting, gnawing worldly care, and turn the sneer of the profane into the worship of the devout, and melt even a heart of stone! This her son, who is not one of our preachers, having no gift that way, and who, like you, doth not much affect the ministry of women, can tell you what her preaching was like; and I will say for him, that he is too sterling a lad to overpraise beyond his judgment even the good mother who bore him."

Thus appealed to, the young man spoke without hesitation and reluctance, and, as it seemed, without favour. "It is true what my father says. ᛫ My mother's sermons were most sweet and suitable. I have known few weary of her discourse, and few who were not the better for it. Other women appear to me to wax weak and distempered, and to utter frothy matter, or to repeat themselves; but my mother was more reasonable, collected, and concise, as well as more earnest, genuine, and heavenly-minded, when she was carried away with her theme, than any speaker I have ever heard; unless it be one whom truth and not flattery compels me to except—yourself, sir, in your happy moments; for you know I have not lived long enough to have ever heard Mr. John Wesley, or Fletcher, or Whitfield, or any of those you term our Boanerges."

"No, boy. But I fall far short of your mother; I come not near her, though I have had so many more years of grace given me, and so many more years of the practice of preaching, and though you, being her boy as well as mine, and spoilt by her in that respect, wise as she was, are too prone to exalt me."

"And yet, with two such qualified progenitors, you do not attempt the public speaking yourself, my young sir," speculated

Monsieur, a little mockingly; "'tis a rare continence."

"I am not fit for it," declared the young Squire, with a straightforwardness which wholly disarmed superciliousness; "I do not wear the Methodists' dress because it would be hypocrisy in me, who have not come out of the world as they have done, nor, indeed, am persuaded that their peculiar separation from the world ought to be mine also. I am good for nothing but to take care of my father's beast when he forgets that he carries a student and a preacher, and is like to stumble and throw his rider; or to knock down any man who lays a rough hand on a godly, beneficent man, be he a squire like my father, or a poor journeyman shoemaker, a brother of St. Crispin, as my father calleth him, which so many of our travelling preachers are—whether there be Methodism in the smell of the leather, or any other provoking cause, I wot not."

"My lad, let not the devil cause thee to bear false witness, even though it be in decrying thyself. Thou art eyes to the blind, and feet to the lame, for my eyes were never good for much but poring over brown books, or peering closely into men's faces, or scanning far off the vague vast of the sky; and my feet hath my father's old punishment of gout in them."

"Though you gave up tea and coffee as too stimulating and pampering, along with my mother and Mr. John Wesley, a score of years agone," commented the son.

"And you profess to keep the farming of the old Mall within bounds, when you pretend that the agriculture of Virgil is wrong?"

"So it is, sir," argued the young Squire, stoutly; "when you apply what was written for Northern Italy, under the Romans, to

Midland England under the house of Brunswick."

"Do not you read Virgil also, my young sir?" inquired Grand'mère, inquisitively.

"No, madam, I am too thick of the head, and have too much to occupy and divert me at present. Perhaps I shall turn to it when my brains have grown with use, or when other trades fail; when I am disabled for the active duties and diversions for which I am persuaded I am designed at present, which my father doth not forbid, and in which I do not see any harm."

"Yea; let every man be fully persuaded in his own mind," murmured Caleb Gage the elder, "for there are divers operations, but the same Spirit."

In the meantime young Caleb Gage had been trying to make himself agreeable to the Dupuys, and to improve the acquaintance of Yolande Dupuy, just as he would have done with a companion of his sisters, had he had sisters. He had tried it in various ways, and had at last retired foiled from the effort. He had got, in reply to his queries, which should have interested any ordinary young girl, the briefest monosyllables. Whether she liked Sedge Pond and its neighbourhood?—Whether she had been in the Castle Gardens?—Whether she were given to the rearing and teaching of tame birds, as he had heard tell French women were, and in that case whether she would care to have birds snared for her? or whether she were minded to have the pond dredged? These, and such as these, were the questions with which Caleb Gage plied Yolande unsuccessfully. But he was left utterly uncertain whether Ma'mselle was a stone statue of a proper young gentlewoman, as she sat there in her silk sacque and her great bow of rose riband on her cap, a tinge of rose coming into her white cheeks for a second, and then leaving them again, just to show that she was really living flesh, and not dead marble; or whether in her superior learning she scorned him.

The truth was that Yolande, as Grand'-mère had seen, was more ignorant of the world, more strange to its ways, and more at a loss what to say and do than any girl just out of her convent. She had hardly seen or spoken to any man save her father's associates in trade, who had not treated her as an equal, but as a child. She was certainly glad enough that anybody should think so kindly of them as to visit them. But she did not know what to make of the young Squire's rank freedom; and could not tell whether it was right for him to address her as he did, or whether he would presume to address Dorothy and Camilla

Rolle with such ease, and whether they would suffer it.

The visitors were invited to share in a meal with the inmates of the Cottage, and this invitation they accepted with polite alacrity, and without any objections, save that Squire Gage quietly declined to drink healths, saying that he had prayed for the company already, and would pray for and with them again whenever they liked, but that neither he nor any other Methodist would pledge a bumper, any more than they would pour out a libation. Shortly after the meal was over, father and son took their departure.

The Gages had inspired a sentiment in the inmates of the Cottage more akin to good will than the Rolles had been able to do on first acquaintance. Grand'mère was especially pleased with them, and was not guiltless of forming her own projects and building her own castles in the air, even on so short an acquaintance—projects in which the Gages, father and son, figured largely.

"Grand'mère," interrupted Yolande, "did you observe Mr. Gage's eyes, which are short-sighted? They are like nothing but the evening star when the dew is falling."

"Yes, little one, and I have seen eyes like them in the long past; eyes with a short sight for the present, and a far sight for the future. No marvel that they are both unfathomable and effulgent, for they have done as great things as the Italian who went down into the Inferno—they have looked into eternity, these eyes, and it is reflected in their glance."

CHAPTER VIII.

Grand'mère turns Miser—An Embassy to the Mall—Sortes Biblicæ.

GRAND'MÈRE, with all her inward peace, had a care on her mind, the more imperative that it was tender. But after the Gages had introduced themselves at the Shottery Cottage, she did not so much shake off the care as find that the solution of the problem took a tangible shape, and became to her sanguine temper and ardent imagination more and more practicable and probable.

Then Grand'mère sought with some formality a special interview with Monsieur, her son, and communicated her intentions to him.

Monsieur laughed a little, even at his mother, in this case, for Grand'mère's care bulked so slightly in his mind, that it appeared a very bagatelle, weighed in the scale against his obligations. But he admitted there was some foundation for her concern, and he gave his mother *carte blanche* to do what she could to remove the cause.

"I leave it to you, *ma mère;* it is your affair. I believe these are honest people, and the *liaison* may be agreeable to them (since there is no inequality of fortune, when they have wasted the better part of their patrimony on alms-deeds) for the sake of you, little mother, and their hero—this Monsieur, I do not know who—Fléchier. As to the *tourterelle*, she may do as well with them as with others. She abuses the

English, that poor child; but she has not even the *débonnaireté* of these *drôles* the pastor's daughters. Psch! Yolande's blood is cold, and her colour grey, like the English climate and sky, which I do not abuse; she has the spleen, the unfortunate! the English form of the excellent mother's faith—*tristesse*, chagrin. Is it not true, my mother?"

"All the waters run to the river, my son," replied Grand'mère, with a shade of impatience and indignation. "Whom should the child resemble unless her near relations? But she is a good child, a noble child, word of mine, Hubert. There are men and women who know their kind, that would give more for the truth, and for the earnestness, all sombre as yet, of our Yolande, than for the light, treacherous frivolity, and the natures all egotism and all passion, of the girls of the world."

"*Ouais!* She is severe. I have never heard her called so before. The nursling is very near thy heart, Grand'mère."

"Because you have a diamond, and you do not know it, papa Dupuy. You embark what remains of your good head and heart in ventures and schemes alone. The good Philippine is not altogether wrong. Yet you have bread, and *fripe* also, already. You are better off than most of our *emigrés*, and you cannot even spare time to get a glimpse of your diamond, though you are aware that it is the pure and precious diamond, which is rough and dark in the mine, till it is brought to the light and cut, ready to be set in the crown of the king."

"I have had a diamond all my days, my old woman, cut and polished before I ever looked upon it; and it is not true that I have not noticed it, and valued it, when it alone had sent radiance into the dark places thousands of times. But I am too old, too *bourgeois*, and have yet too many rivals to overcome in trade, which is my calling, to want another diamond, or to cut it for myself; and you women, born *religieuses*, will not understand such things. I shall take it on trust, if you please, and I shall leave you to dispose of it, to bestow it to shine (poor little diamond! the sun to it, with all my heart) in another house, and show myself the son of my mother in this liberality—and I cannot help that defect altogether, since I happen to be one of the rude, hard, worldly *bêtes* of men whom poor Philippine rails at. Go! let her rail, if it does her good, what does it signify?"

Grand'mère bade Yolande go and aid big Priscille, as she wished to speak with her mother; and she consulted Madame so soon as Monsieur had retired to his study, or rather his business-room.

And Madame said she did not love the English; she did not trust them; she would rather see the mortal remains of Yolande in English earth than that the immortal spirit of the child should forget and forsake the faith of the French soil, for which her ancestors had watered the land with their best blood. As to Lutheranism, it was a *tantamarre* of Protestantism; Methodism might be better, but she did not like the tree on which the fruit grew. At the same time, it was true that a girl could not be left alone to face the dangers and the temptations of the world. There were no French parents who would not seek in good time the protection of another's house and home for a young maiden. Monsieur would bring them all to the Bastille of England, or to the horse-pond, some day. Ah! she begged Grand'mère's pardon for speaking disrespectfully of her son. She had forgotten for the moment that her husband was Grand'-mère's son, and *petite mère* should not go to the Bastille. She was too venerable, too near the saints. *Petite mère* should go with Yolande. Monsieur would not allow it otherwise, and she would not allow it; for it would be undutiful and unkind to the dear old mother. No, she alone would accompany Monsieur, and perhaps the sooner the better, if it brought him to a right mind, to faith and repentance.

"My Philippine, thou art honourable and devout to the finger tips; but thou art not a trooper. No! thou art weak as water, with the throes of passion, like many another poor woman, my child. If thou wouldst only have faith in the good God, and fervent charity towards men," adjured Grand'mère, with commiseration. "But nevertheless chagrin is in the humours of the blood, my love, I believe it well; and when we judge harshly, very often we should do better to have great pity."

Madame would have infinitely preferred to transplant Yolande into a French household, but at Sedge Pond the Dupuys were isolated from their countrymen, save in the case of those business men whom Madame looked upon as denaturalised renegades, the accomplices of Monsieur's Mammon-worship and plotting ambition. Then there was just enough of the *bourgeoise* in Madame to be sensible of the disadvantage of having bread without *fripe*, as was true of the mass of the Huguenot *emigrés*, and the consequent temptation when bread and *fripe* were offered to them to lick the *fripe* on their own account, and, so far as faithful regard and abiding friendship were concerned, leave the bread to take its own chance, and to be trampled under foot in the crowd of other relations and interests. Thus while Madame groaned in spirit, as she did over most proposals which were made to her, she saw no reason for treating what had the great weight of Grand'mère's wish as rank apostasy and villainy.

Thus Grand'mère, in her sweet cracked voice, began to sing, over her cooking, distilling, lace-weaving, not Clement Marot's psalms alone, though she sang them oftenest and with most satisfaction, but old ballads and folk-songs, which were like drops of the nation's heart, that she had never despised and never forgotten, and which now came to her, in green, misty England, with touches of the varied colours and wafts of the sweet odours of the south.

Grand'mère also suddenly developed a passion for coins, especially for gold pieces—canary birds, as she called them. She was evidently making a collection of them, and hoarding as many sovereigns as she could come by. When Yolande sought the reason of this, Grand'mère put her off with the pleasantry that she was becoming avaricious in her old age, and was scraping together a "little fortune to leave Yolande an heiress."

But Grand'mère made a bad miser, for Priscille came in and told her a sad story of a poor spendthrift prodigal gentleman, a stranger, who had come with his wife, a forlorn fine lady, and hidden their heads from the shame of witnessing an execution in their own house, under the roof of the ale-house of Sedge Pond. They were not able to go any further, or try any new mode of life, because they had not the money to pay for their entertainment, and they were now in such a strait that the gentleman had threatened to hang or drown himself. Then Grand'mère stole secretly out, with the help of Madame Rougeole, solicited the honour of being allowed to wait on the couple, and proposed, in a roundabout, ingenious way, to offer them a little loan, as if it were an agreeable scheme of putting out at interest a portion of her thousands of spare francs and crowns. On the strength of this loan she was privileged to see the helpless couple go away in the coach, to throw themselves on the much-tried mercy of such older, wiser, and better supplied friends as might be left to them, but with small prospect to Grand'mère of ever seeing her canary birds again.

Grand'mère's indemnification was the half-affronted recollection of how the theatrical, fine gentleman, with his unpowdered hair hanging like candle-wicks over his face, and his velvet coat stained and soiled, had wished to kneel to her, and she had quickly prevented him:

"No, sir, kneel to your God."

And when he had stared, looked foolish,

and shrugged his shoulders, she had been compelled to cry,

"Do you not know him? Have you never kneeled to Him? What marvel that everything has gone wrong with you, even till you have come to perish with hunger?"

Afterwards the fellow had insisted on kissing Grand'mère's hand, and vowed that as she had done more for him than all his friends among the quality, for her sake he would never bet, or game, or race, or swear more, strike him dead if he would.

And Grand'mère stopped her ears, put her hand on his bold mouth, and cried dolefully to the prodigal, who was not yet five-and-twenty—

"If thou canst not keep thyself from sin for God's sake and thine own, how thinkest thou that thou canst have strength to do it for the sake of an old Huguenot? Nay, leave off these big promises, and look to thy wife, whom thou hast taught to game and bet as furiously as thyself. Behold the cards and spadille hidden in thy cuff, as if that were thy chief care and the work for thy last moments; and I heard her wagering the lace of her cap against the braid of your coat that I was the hostess come to crave you again, as I mounted the stairs. She is frightened to contradict you, I see it in her eyes, but she shrinks from starvation and infamy, and from lawless violence. Oh! do you not, my *pauvrette?* Then go, my *mirliflore* of a debtor, and promise to me not at all, but perform a little to save that lost child whom thou hast helped to drag to the brink of the precipice. Yet, not even for her, no, not even for her, wilt thou pause and think, and play the man before it is too late, unless thou canst arise and go to thy Father."

The sinner went at last, his head hanging

a little. It was exceedingly doubtful, however, whether, unless in the exhaustless hopefulness of Grand'mère, he would not be sneering at her before he had turned the corner. "But what of that?" Grand'mère would have asked. "Behold the dark silent night, when he may think better of it. Behold the moments of trial, anguish, terror, alas! alas! coming thick and fast on such as he, when, while there is still mercy for him, he may recall even so poor a lesson."

Grand'mère returned to the Shottery Cottage, and looked a little ruefully at her empty purse, the canaries all fled from it. Eventually she consoled herself with the simple reflection that money was one thing, and men and women another; and that failing the gold there was always the copper, which was only a metal a little redder in colour and heavier in weight. If Yolande could not have a dozen louis in her pocket one day, she might have a dozen of dozen of sous, which would be a great deal grander in point of number, for the sake of her dear old France and its discreet, economical country customs.

Yolande, girl as she was, had her thoughts and suspicions in the middle of her constant questioning, pondering, and disputing; but they were single-hearted, submissive, and child-like. And when the crisis arrived for Grand'mère to make known her intention of going alone on an expedition to the Mall, to return the visit of Squire Gage, Yolande cast down her eyes, shrank a little more into herself, looked colder and graver in tone, and more nervous and timid, a new phase of her quietness and gravity; but she did not dream of so much as suggesting opposition to Grand'mère's enterprise. There would have been indelicacy and insubordination, even according to Grand'mère's standard, in such a step on Yolande's part.

Grand'mère had had so few opportunities of visiting, and had so seldom availed herself of them for many years, that she declared it made her old head light, when she started on one of the Rector's horses, which was borrowed for the occasion. Madame Rolle had offered the use of her chariot, but Grand'mère had that honourable pride which would have nothing to do with what was out of keeping with her real position. She was an old *bourgeoise* Huguenot; her pride, so far as it was permissible, lay in that distinction. She did not care to be rolling, or rather bumping heavily along the bad roads, like the quality. She accepted the attendance of Black Jasper, however, because she wanted a man to walk by her horse. She thought it would be a mutual advantage, and a kind of treat to the poor fellow, who wore a bit of crape for

Captain Philip round his arm soldier-wise, which he had begged one of the Rectory still-maids to sew on for him; and he never passed the Rector without trying to cover it clumsily with his hand, or his hat, or his napkin, as if that would cover a father's grief. He never glanced at it himself without his rolling eyes getting dim. But if Grand'mère was as elated as a child at her new circumstances, she had a child's generosity in seeking to share them with her neighbours. She desired to do Priscille's business and the business of every other house-wife who would trust her, at the wheel-wright's and the miller's on the road. She sat equipped for starting full ten minutes, to allow Black Jasper to enjoy the spectacle of a man and an ape performing before the ale-house porch.

At last Grand'mère set out to ride her six miles, and back. On she went by the

Waäste, past an occasional windmill, which struck her as being the likest feature to France in the landscape; on by another rural village much in the style of Sedge Pond. She passed farm-houses, confused masses of out-buildings, only a little less sluttish than the villages, forsaken by their occupants for the harvest-work in the fields. She got gleams of the great white stuccoed arcade of the Rolles' castle, which carried the rampant imagination of Grand'mère to the Louvre at the least. And always journeying with her there was the same slow, sleepy river, like a canal, bearing a barge or two, bound for Norwich.

Grand'mère and Black Jasper travelled in the greatest harmony. They were not without annoyances, however. The children of the strange village, who had never seen a black servant before, but who had, nevertheless, arrived at the conclusion that his name was Black-a-more, came out and stared, pointed their fingers, screamed, and mocked at Black Jasper, who was naturally oppressed by these attentions; and the little gall that was in him being roused, he made faces, and threatened the small fry in hurried, impressive pantomime.

"Seest thou not, my son, that it is of no use? Thou attractest them only the more. Heed them not. If they did not stare and and shout at thee, they would stare and shout at me—at my French tongue, at the fashion of my grey hair, and the cut of my mantua."

Black Jasper ruminated on the beautiful old lady's calling him her son, and comparing him to herself; and became so inflated with conceit, that the next time he was assailed by his too ardent admirers, he raised his cocked hat, made a low bow, and then spreading out his sable fingers on his white shirt, saluted their tips till the children cried, "Boo! boo! lulliberoo!" more loudly and frantically than ever, and Grand'mère, it must be confessed, was slightly scandalized at her train.

The Mall was a square building of red brick with white facings, like a soldier's uniform of scarlet cloth and pipe-clay. It had not only done good private service in its day—had not only held in its oak and cedar parlours whole generations of the Gages from the reign of Anne, and had hidden priests of all denominations in the hole behind the chimney of the dining-hall, which was a fragment of an older building—but it had seen public service lately. It was an old seat in the modest rank of English country mansions, and it was a Methodist establishment, combining college (on the principle of Kingswood), orphanage, hospice for belated travellers, hospital for the helpless sick, and house of refuge for the homeless poor. All its buildings and pleasure-grounds, which were not absolutely required in the economy of its large household, were transformed from their original aims, and pressed into the use of a motley regiment. The hall was a meeting-house and class-room, where preachers and teachers lectured and taught; the stable was almost stripped of its stalls, while the loft above was fitted up into humble dormitories. The coach-house was the hospital, and an old berline which still stood in a corner served as the refractory ward for an occasional violent patient. The kennels were workshops, in which travelling tailors, shoemakers, and basket-makers made periodical sojourns, and found apprentices ready to their hands; while a company of young girls was distributed, under capable, vigilant matrons, over the kitchen, the wash-house, the bake-house, the dairy, and the housekeeper's room. In addition to the Methodist preachers, in every degree of training, whom Squire Gage housed, fed, clad, sent out and followed with never-failing interest into their circuits of evangelisation, the Mall was well stocked with poor relations, who chose to make it their head-quarters on the right of charity's beginning at home. The only stipulation with them was that they should attend the exercises, comply with the regulations of the house, and conduct themselves with propriety while they were under its roof. Along with the regular pensioners Squire Gage took in an irregular band. Any number of chance wayfarers, who preferred a dish of groats and a crust with a grace said to it, clean straw, and the shelter of a roof, to the highway, a grudged shed, and the pence demanded for the humblest supper and bed at the ale-house, were also taken in at the Mall and made welcome.

Thus Grand'mère did not find the country house, basking sluggishly in the afternoon sun, solitary, save for its two masters and their domestics; on the contrary, it overflowed with life in all ranks and at all stages. From a waggon before the porch, two little boys, in corduroys and knee-breeches, were just alighting. They had rusty bands of crape round their bonnets, and were very thin-faced and watery-eyed—a consignment a brother Methodist in the next large town had sent to fill up two vacancies in Brother Gage's orphanage. There was a figure wrapped in a blanket, and taken straight to the hospital, as like to be a patient in small-pox as anything else. There was a halt man in a frieze coat; a blind woman in a duffle cloak, with the hood drawn over her head; and a scarecrow of an old gentlewoman, in a gipsy bonnet and a *roquelaure*, claiming remote kindred with Squire Gage, and cumbered with so many trunks and band-boxes that she certainly meant to push her claim to the extent of spending the remainder of her days at the Mall, while she looked sourly at the halt and the blind, as if dreading that there might not be bread enough and to spare for her and for them. There were all imaginable noises, the sound of planes, saws, resined strings, and voices from the workshop.

Elderly women and half-grown girls, precise, and only curbed in their sauciness, were moving to and fro in the porch, at the windows of the house, and on the landing-places of the outside stairs, engaged in scouring, mending, preparing meals, attending to the dumb animals, and waiting on those who could not wait on themselves. A beggar was examining his wallet; a hawker sorting his stock of ballads; an old soldier was airing his patched and faded uniform, a scar on his wrinkled forehead. But each was at his ease, and exhibited an inclination to growl at and grudge elbow-room to his neighbour in the ivied court. Itinerant preachers, in the elevation of their calling, were studying, by the help of books and papers, apart from the throng, or discussing together for the most part doctrines, creeds, and experiences, sometimes with a war of words rising, ebbing, raging, falling. Students and disputants paced up and down, and rested in the walks, arbours, and summer-houses of what had once been the gardens in which the ladies of the Mall had taken delight, while the men had rejoiced in their hunters and harriers, their hunting breakfasts and coursing dinners. The late Dame Gage, though she had loved flowers with the best flower-lovers among her predecessors, had voluntarily and cheerfully given over her garden to pass into the commonest of kitchen and of physic gardens, for the behoof of the great family at the Mall. Only here and there, a tiger-lily or a nectarine yet struggled into stately gorgeous flower or luscious fruit, like plants of another age and region, among coarse beans and cabbages, chamomiles and horehound, gnarled crabs and plums. And Grand'mère hailed a huge walnut-tree, which continued to shade one corner; and she hung over the straggling tendrils and leaves of a wilding vine, for it was such as she had known grow trim and fair and fruitful in hundreds of tender green, olive, and straw-coloured saplings in her vineyard in Languedoc.

She looked round without misgiving, and with sympathetic interest in the extraordinary colony. When Squire Gage was apprised of her arrival, he hastened to welcome her with the warmest cordiality, and received her with the greatest honour. He, however, had no other apartment to which to conduct her, save kitchen and parlour in one, where elm-wood dresser, birch-wood settles, cherry-wood cupboards, pewter flagons, box-wood bowls, and dishes of coarsest earthenwere, did duty for fine furniture, and which was the only company room left at the Mall. Grand'mère looked round her with more than perfect acquiescence—with glad approval. She trod like a queen on a progress, when Mr. Gage led her, after she had rested, over his wonderful human laboratory. She went with him into what he called the academicia, into the porticoes, the hall, and the garden, and heard him help aspiring boys, sons of poor Nonconformist ministers and schoolmasters, to construe Sallust and solve Euclid, as they had begun to do in the intervals of "lashing" out the corn on the shelling hill, and walking in the furrow of the plough at their homes. She saw him pull the locks of others, and bid them not smuggle away their "Seven Champions" and "Robinson Crusoes," for his good brother Adam Clarke had demonstrated beyond contradiction that from nursery fairy tales and school-boy legends he had learnt what had served to help his faith in the invisible, and to teach him to endure hardness as a good soldier of the greatest and best of Lords. He took Grand'mère from workshop to hospital, charming her by his unconscious power of wisdom and love in their management; and she delighted him by disarming the hostility of the crowd of performers whom his hand—practised in blessing—ruled harmoniously, but who were liable to prove unruly and contentious under any other leader, and to resent keenly the suspicion of an interloper. But Grand'mère praised right and left in all good will, first frankly acknowledging the merits of sorrel salve and elderberry wine, of goose pie and blackberry pudding, and then she presented a box of French unguent for wounds and bruises, and a case of cassia; finally she begged a saucepan, six beaten eggs, six bits of butter the size of a nut (telling them the French cook's proverb was, " Spare neither butter nor care "), a little shredded basil and thyme, and a little grated ham, a pinch of pepper and salt, and tossed in a trice before their eyes that "*omelette aux fines herbes*," the very naming of which is sufficient to improvise an appetite in the sickliest of convalescents.

But there were other relics of the original gentle estate and destination of the Mall, beyond its stone and wood work. The principal of these were the books of its master's library, in the ancient dignity of vellum and calf's-skin, still stored in book-cases at one end of the kitchen; and the family pictures, which yet looked strangely down, in the pink of proud and affected attitudes and attire, from a high white-washed open gallery running round the room, on the bustle below.

Squire Gage explained that he had once entertained serious thoughts of burning his books, as the hearers of the Apostle Paul did theirs; or, at least, of selling them like other luxuries, for what money they would bring into the treasury of the establishment. But then, again, he had considered that his old friends and faithful companions contained no magical arts, and he had spared them, as he was thankful for afterwards. The longer he lived, the more fully he was assured that a man should be thoroughly furnished to every good work, and that there was no furnishing, after the inspiration of the Spirit and the teaching of Holy Scripture, which was to be compared with the clouded, corrupted wisdom of the ancients, so that a man's eye was purged to see through the dimness of their vision. And if a man's eye remained without light, why then both the wisdom and the folly of the ancients and the moderns would be all one to him in his darkness. His lad, indeed, did not at present affect the classics, nor yet, save in a modified degree, the English authors themselves. But what of that?— one man's meat was another man's poison; there were other lads to whom he could lay open his library, and to whom Caleb would never grudge the beauty and the wealth of his father's grand old books.

As to the pictures, there were brethren who remonstrated with Squire Gage for keeping them in their bare canvas, in the manner in which they had hung since his dame freed them from their frames, which she had dispatched, along with what plate, tapestry, ebony, ivory, silk and fine linen there had been at the Mall, to be disposed of in London, to help the funds for the systematic relief of one small fraction of the poor and needy. These strict brethren were apprehensive lest the poor painted faces, lovelocks, top-knots, sword-hilts and citherns should serve to produce pride of birth and race in their possessor. But though the Squire protested gravely that he did not think it was asked of him, or of any man, to sit in judgment on the sins of his forefathers, and "improve" them, he was of opinion that there was as much humility as pride to be got from the honest study of those lingering shadows on the wall. And the Squire, as he spoke, glanced at a truculent old Gage who had done great execution in the Civil Wars, and a vain, light woman who had wedded and abandoned him.

"But tell me, my Monsieur," asked Grand'mère, thoughtfully, as she inspected his labours, "will this gracious house last? Is it that you have founded it in perpetuity, or that the benevolent will keep it up by a succession of donations and dedications, as in the French houses of charity and mercy? Pardon me, Monsieur, that I am a Lot's wife of doubt and distrust, and fear that the Mall house may be abused like other houses in other hands, and in other generations. How will you guard and fence it when even the brave young Monsieur is done with carrying out his father's intentions?"

Squire Gage smiled gently, and shook his head. "It is one good of imperfection, madam, that it wants not fencing and guarding. And that this poor scheme of mine is imperfect, I and my dame knew from the beginning. But what would you have? There was a crying need for some reformation, some commencement of a good work. We made our trial, and did our best—for our day. My dear madam, a future day is not mine, and I am not called upon to provide for it, or meddle with it. No, I shall not bequeath the rents which may yet come in to me to Gage's Hospital. Why should I? God has raised a natural barrier. My lad is as much a messenger from Him, and the messenger who comes first and nearest to me, as my poorest fellow-creature."

"And Monsieur Caleb, will he not wash the disciples' feet also?"

"Not in his father's and mother's way. Why should he? There is no call upon him to walk in their footsteps. He may go his own way. Any other conclusion savoureth of an automaton and a martinet, since my son is not of the stuff which hypocrites are made of. No, he may go his own way, so that he follow in Another's footsteps; and how far and wide they diverge, on how many soils, by how many paths, blessed be God, do these divinely human footsteps travel! I go thus far, that I have not, in my opinion, made Caleb a poorer man in the long run, because I have spent the savings of my minority, besides some furnishings and personal belongings, and sold a farm or two, which might have fallen to him. He will have enough for a gentleman farmer. He may take in land, rear stock, buy and sell, build up the house anew, extend its borders, for he is shrewd and prudent, and skilful in business, as well as generous and modest. He may break up the Waüste, drain the Mall Deep, cut down the old coppice, erect woolmills and cornmills just as the first Gage of the Mall drew the first furrow between this and Sedge Pond. It is in the kind, and in the sample, and thence we have been distinguished as namesakes of the son of Jephunneh, who had the hill-country of Hebron for his portion, and the expulsion of the sons of Anak for his reward. Nay, but forgive this foolish boasting; it is an old man's garrulity. Caleb will not continue the establishment; but I have confidence in my son that he will let it go down slowly and gently, and that he will not be minded to turn the last of its inmates adrift; not though he were the most troublesome and ingrained black sheep. He will honour the Methodist body that far, and none the less esteem it that he hath never belonged to it; and he will not be in any haste to remove his father and mother's landmarks."

"It is true, my friend," replied Grand'-mère, "that there are Christians, and Christians; and I confess it does seem to me that the early Christians selling their land, laying the money at the Apostles' feet, and having all their goods in common, reads like practices designed for the exigencies of their country and age, not as a pattern for all time."

"Without doubt, my dear madam; and young eyes see flaws in goodly robes which their predecessors wore with exultation and thankfulness. Why not? What were the clearness and sunshine of the present given them for, if not to correct what is cumbrous and obsolete, unfit and misshapen in the cloak or gown, though it served its turn in days gone by, when no fault was seen in it and it sheltered its wearer from the mists and storms of the winter of the past. I have always thought it one of the inconsistencies and eccentricities of your Michel de Montaigne that he would go abroad in his father's old cloak because it was his father's. Caleb doth not choose to vex me, but I know he thinks my large family cannot last long (inasmuch as it is an arbitrary institution, and not God's ordinance of blood and kindred), when there is no supreme necessity for it, without breeding and fostering jealousies, strife, and violence, as in the religious houses of all sects, after a lapse of time. The boy hath had before now to help me to put down differences and divisions, even between preachers and teachers, with a high hand, and once we had to call in the civil power against a poor rogue of a tinker who had reminded me of a certain illustrious dreamer, but who was unlike John Bunyan in this respect, that he was so left to himself as to take all he could get and give the worst word on his entertainment, annoy and insult his fellow-lodgers, and drive them from receiving profit from the exercises. At last he sunk to the low pitch of lusting after the very homely trenchers and porringers out of which he had eaten his meals, and of secreting them with the purpose of removing them. My good dame, he struck and kicked the man who detected him in his iniquity so forcibly, that murder might have been done had not Caleb, in his young strength and natural bravery, gone between and sundered the combatants. Yet, if you will believe it, that poor sinner wept abundantly when he made full confession to me in Reedham Gaol, and declared, what I have no reason to discredit, that he was never so near grace as in his earlier sojourn at the Mall. Therefore, why should not grace surprise some other wretched wayfarer any day before I draw my last breath at the Mall—come upon him like a strong man, take from him his goods and deprive him of his armour wherein he trusted, and leave him not with the dismal wail 'almost,' but the jubilant shout, 'altogether a Christian?'"

"Monsieur," cried Grand'mère, impulsively, as she raised her grey eyes to his violet eyes, "I am older than you, but I am a weak, foolish woman; grant me a favour,—give me your blessing."

"All the blessings of the heaven above and the earth beneath!" responded Squire Gage, fervently; "though they are called down by an unworthy brother on a true sister. Rather, I should beg a Huguenot's prayers for me and mine, and for my work, which is nearly ended. Shall we pray together, madam?"

In this manner two Christian enthusiasts pondered on Christian ethics, compared notes on good works, and thought no shame of reverently approaching their Father in heaven.

The Squire was solicitous, with a country gentleman's imperative hospitality, to entertain Grand'mère as became both her and him. With a delicate tenderness of respect he had even striven to recall old memories, and to send his usual habits to the wall for the occasion, so that the meal served at one end of the kitchen, with its fruit, white wine, and the nosegay of all the autumn flowers then blowing in Dame Lucy's disenfranchised parterres, should be as like as possible to the French feast which he had once seen served up, in an English parsonage, by the quick instincts of a soul as generous as his own.

Grand'mère received every gracious attention with a gratitude and a gratification still more gracious.

"Monsieur," she exclaimed, in her lively, metaphorical way, looking round on the tankards, the books, the pictures, and the banquet, with eyes which would never grow too dim to sparkle, "it is as if you had got cray-fish from Montfaucon, wild boars from

Ardennes, fierce bears from the Pyrenees. It is as if you had received an intimation that the three Magi were coming to visit you, and had made your preparations accordingly."

The young Squire was from home, which was only a partial disappointment to Grand'-mère, since it was one part of her intention to make the most searching, interested inquiries, which her perfect politeness would permit, respecting the disposition and inclination of Monsieur Caleb.

In truth, very little importunity was needed in order to obtain the desired information, for here "the old man eloquent" was full of very pardonable fatherly garrulity. His son Caleb was his first and last born—his only child, the son of Rachel, the prop of his old age, the desire of his fading eyes. He christened him without fear as the gift of God, and beheld in their relationship, not only the opportunity for the lawful indulgence of his natural affections, but the type of all that is tender and true, loyal and sacred, binding the creature to the Creator, the manifold children to the universal Father.

It sounded as if the father and the son were not only filial, but fraternal in their regard, as if they were a pair of close friends, such as two good men living alone together in a circle of dependents might well become. Yet this freedom and familiarity disturbed Grand'mère's calculations a little. Squire Gage not only expatiated contentedly on the assistance which his son rendered him, and the confidence which he reposed in him; but he recounted gleefully the vigorous, stubborn mental encounters the two had on the subjects wherein they differed; the lessons they gave each other in opposite sciences, and the news with which they twitted each other on their failures. Grand'mère was actually tempted to hold up her hands and cry halt. She could hardly fathom such a relationship; she had been accustomed to playful as well as tender friendship between mother and son, but between father and son, even where there was devoted affection, she had witnessed no such liberty. It required Grand'mère's forbearance and her liking for the family at the Mall to look over this dangerous license, and make her attribute it to English air and English institutions alone.

Having subdued this single scruple, Grand'mère came at last to the object of her mission, not without *finesse* and circumlocution; because, though her character was in essentials clear as crystal, it included in its elements delicate French tact and ingenuity. The substance of the errand was quite simple: Grand'mère had a grand-daughter,

Squire Gage had a son, and the promising young man and young woman, both moderately endowed with the goods of fortune, were contemporaries and neighbours: was there no significance, no suitability in these things? Grand'mère made a proposal of a treaty of marriage between the Squire's son and her grand-daughter, Yolande Dupuy. She had no notion that she was doing anything but conferring the highest honour by the overture, while it was a matter of course that it should come from her. She was fully persuaded that the Squire and she were the persons strictly entitled to settle the preliminaries of any matrimonial alliance entered into by their children, and that no one, not even the principals, could be more deeply interested or more sensible of the importance of the step suggested. Grand'mère, therefore, spoke with quiet dignity and with a due consciousness of her authority in the matter.

The Squire was somewhat taken aback as Grand'mère; in fairness to her grand-child, fluently, but without exaggeration, summed up briefly the advantages of the match, dwelling on Yolande's good qualities, her virtue and wisdom, her truth to her parents, and her sweetness to her Grand'mère. The comparatively innocent seclusion in which she had grown up, the fitting instruction she had received, the personal attractions (though these were but a *bagatelle*) that she possessed, and the modest but respectable dowry which her father was able and willing to give her, all these were faithfully touched on. Then Grand'mère went nimbly over to the other side of the question, and dwelt nobly, liberally, and at far greater length, on the merits of the young Squire, in his reputation, his family, his *ménage*. Yolande's father and mother would do their utmost to meet the young man's gifts with their Yolande's goodness. They wished to marry their daughter while they could still choose for her in marriage, and give her hand where there was least risk of a fatal error. And Squire Gage, who was a father, would not blame them or scorn them because they were foreigners and French.

The Squire was not altogether so confounded as a modern, learned, and devout squire—did such exist—might be now-a-days. Marriages continued frequently to be family alliances in houses far below the rank of those of dukes and earls. Squire Gage's father had found his wife selected, sought out, and all but married to him by an obliging and active-minded kinswoman, and the Squire had never had any reason to regard his father and mother as other than a well matched, well satisfied couple. The early Methodists were accustomed to view wedlock with a strong reference to the interests of the society. In this light influential members, without hesitation or fear, arranged and carried through marriages for the good of the meeting-house or chapel first, the individuals' claims and characters being glanced at afterwards. Some of the obscurer conferences might even occasionally decide them by lot, like the Moravians. Squire Gage remembered that it had been an obstacle to his own union, and regarded as a serious difficulty and danger, that it had taken its rise in the motions of carnal affection and the promptings of the natural man, and not in a single eye to the evangelisation of the world, and a profound respect for the extension of Christianity.

So Squire Gage was not inclined to silence or scout Grand'mère's mission, even if his goodness had suffered him to be hasty in condemning and deriding what had been undertaken in good faith and sober earnestness. He consented to take the proposal into mature consideration without a thought of doing any wrong to his friend and son. He freely admitted that he would rejoice to have a young gentlewoman at the Mall again, particularly if she were of Grand'-mère's race and rearing. He was not such a miserable bigot, either to his nation or to his Methodism, as to undervalue the whole French people and the noble band of Huguenot exiles. He confessed there was some call for another mistress at the Mall, though the mention of it brought the rheum to the eyes which had seen its last mistress. But Madam could comprehend and make allowance for that. One who would deal kindly with his infirmities, and would manage the women, amongst whom he and Caleb could not enter and hector to the extent of lending a rough lick to an incorrigible malcontent, would be a great blessing to them. The greatest scolds among the women, poor creatures, were always mild negations to him, but there was more than a suspicion that they were apt to employ their leisure in idle bickerings and petty feuds, which, though not serious, were not seemly or conformable to their faith. They would mind a mistress, especially if she were like his old dame, a dove among barndoor fowls. Certainly, for that and for other reasons Squire Gage would gladly hail his son's early entrance into marriage, which was honourable in all men; but his healthy instinct impelled him to add, gently, in the end, "Nevertheless, my good madam, doth it not strike you that our theme savoureth alarmingly of a *mariage de convenance?*"

"Of what else, Monsieur? and of what can you make a better market than of the noblest sort of *convenance*—fitness, obedience to parents, dutifulness—not of fancy and passion?" demanded Grand'mère, warmly. "Ah! trust me, my Monsieur, when the good choice has been made with prayer and blessing by the careful parents, sacred, chaste, sweet wedded love (all the purer and higher that it is born of duty, and not of desire) will follow without fail in those good and honest hearts on which, and not on their memories alone, is written the substance of their catechism, '*Quelle est la principale fin de la vie?*' and '*Quel est le souverain bien des hommes?*' Fie! Monsieur, would you rather have the boys and the girls madly pursuing, and setting their weak seals blemished to their idle, wandering imaginations?" exclaimed Grand'mère, in such unfeigned horror, that under her *empressement* Squire Gage felt all but convicted of impropriety and indiscretion. "You are

English—and the English, the best of them, love their own wills in the affections," continued Grand'mère, more temperately; "but when every great point is gained, is it that you would cast fancy and passion into the opposite *panier*, and suffer it to weigh down the ass, Monsieur? The marriages of Isaac and Rebekah, of Boaz and Ruth—say what were they but the noblest sort of *mariages de convenance?*"

Squire Gage had been slipping his fingers into his great family Bible to find the entry of his son's birth and baptism in order to show it to Grand'mère, in return for the sight of the certificate of the Protestant baptism of Yolande Dupuy, with which he had been favoured. As he did so he was tempted to have recourse to a practice in favour with the old Methodists—even with Mr. John himself—which was not engaged in lightly, far less irreverently, but which nevertheless had a strange resemblance to the heathen art of divination, christened by a Christian name.

"What think you of the *Sortes Biblicæ,* madam? Shall we try a verse of Holy Scripture, to ascertain what we are putting our hands to?"

Grand'mère acquiesced readily. She was not farther before her age than good Squire Gage, and she had her superstitions as well as her French prejudices. She clasped her hands and leant forward breathlessly, while the Squire put his hand darkly into the closed Book on an unseen verse, and opening it read aloud,

"'My son, despise not the chastening of the Lord, neither be weary of his correction.'

"Well, that is plain sailing," declared Squire Gage, submissively, and even cheerfully, seeing Grand'mère's expressive face fall at the indication. "Whatever may come of our communing—and take note this admonition doth not impugn its good ending—patience is a virtue like to be in request for all concerned. I confess I have always been over-fain to seek relief from present evils. If you please, we will take the matter quietly, dear dame, and permit the young people's hearts to speak, though it were but one word. I do not fear that they will speak forwardly.

CHAPTER IX.

The Secret of the Ride to the Mall—A Woman Despised in her Youth.

GRAND'MÈRE returned in good heart to the Shottery Cottage. Her ride to the Mall had only been the commencement of the preliminaries. She had never dreamt of settling the affair in a single interview; that would not have been according to her notions of discretion. She was pleased with all she had seen at the Mall; with the devotion and charity on a large scale her heart was full. But though Grand'mère talked to Yolande by the hour on the veritable hospice she had visited, and on the beauty of character she saw in its founders, not a word did she say which could make the girl cast down her shy eyes in perplexity and confusion. Grand'mère could, without compunction, institute a treaty of marriage for her grand-daughter, but she would have thought herself the most indelicate of women had she breathed a syllable to the girl, who had her suspicions; and this notwithstanding that they were incessantly together, and full of fond confidences.

Unfortunately she was not so reticent elsewhere. Without a thought of any unwomanliness in her act, Grand'mère considered it but neighbourly to whisper it to Madam Rolle of the Rectory. With all her hopes and cares for her daughters, Madam Rolle had never imagined anything so barefaced as this flagrant instance of French fashions and French morals, and was almost staggered in her esteem for the old Grand-

'mère who had tried to break the storm of her own calamity to her. As Madam Rolle kept nothing from the Rector, she immediately imparted to him this startling bit of news; and in return he asked her to what young men he should propose Dolly and Milly? They must not, however, be ranters and Jacobins, who consorted with blaspheming, foul-mouthed, filthy shoemakers and weavers, compared with whom honest chimney-sweeps were finished gentlemen; for he had made up his mind never to ask a favour from these, not even to rid him of his daughters.

Madam Rolle, like many another madam, was at a loss what to make of her husband's irony, and took refuge in the sympathy and indignation of her daughters. She set them up against their young French friend, who was taking such impudent means to get the better of them, and settle herself, before either of them was suited with a husband and an establishment.

Yolande, poor girl, could not understand why all of a sudden the Rectory girls began, in French *parlance*, "to lift their noses at her," to speak at her, to twit her with what she could not help, and to which she was not as yet formally privy. In the end there was great mischief done; so bad, that it was all but irremediable.

Young Caleb Gage had little or no intercourse with the Rolles. The greatest hardship and danger of his position was, that it wholly isolated him from those of his fellows and equals who were not of his father's way of thinking. It mattered little that Caleb the younger differed in his conclusions from Caleb the elder. Unless the young Squire had been prepared to place himself in utter antagonism to the old father whom he venerated so deeply and loved so dearly, his own moderation and his reaction in favour of general Church standards would have profited him nothing.

Men and women of the present day know little of Methodism, if they do not understand that it was the burthen of a world lying in the grossest wickedness, riot, and wantonness, which drove into vehement protest so many good and honest hearts—drove them into the extravagances of enthusiasm and the excesses of zeal, if, indeed, they were extravagances and excesses. For, to judge correctly of such so-called extravagances and excesses, it is necessary to contrast a house like the Mall—its voluntary relinquishment of the state and attributes of gentle station—with houses where notorious wickedness was daily committed, where the same card-party sat, ate, slept, and woke again, while they gambled away their fathers' lands, their children's bread, and even their wretched wives, for twenty or thirty hours at a stretch. In those days women died prematurely, in agonising pangs, from the poison of white paint; while men were found guilty of forgery and highway robbery, and spirits went into the outer darkness for a set of French tapestry, or Indian paper-hangings, a china baby, or a piece of velvet of a rarely pretty device. If we faithfully compare the free reception and wholesale housing of the indigent and outcast at the Mall with the bitter penury and terrible struggles of men and women ruined by the infamous bubble schemes of the era, or by wildly striving to raise themselves out of their low estate of barbarous ignorance and base depravity, then we will, perhaps, form a fair estimate of the influence of Methodism, not only on the corrupt refinement of men of the world, but on the densely stupid, fatuous, sensual animalism of the poor colliers and pottery-men, down whose grimy faces the tears of penitence, purer than dew-drops and brighter than diamonds, "washed the white channels" of a new and better nature at the pleadings, and strivings, and wrestlings in prayer of Whitfield and his brethren. Do not shrink from thinking of that dissolute world, I beseech you, if you would be simply just to the Methodists, and neither exaggerate their Christianity and their heroism, nor extenuate their mysticism and their lapses from the orthodoxy of this or that great creed. After all, one may be permitted to doubt whether the decided position which the early Methodist leaders took up, and the passionate nature of their testimony, were exaggerated and excessive, in view of the crying evils and the barren latitudinarianism with which they waged war.

These sentences are written in the old sense of apology for what needs no apology in the modern meaning of the word, and in feeble illustration of the causes of the peculiarities of Methodism. Little do modern men and women, for the most part, know of the brand which the early Methodists bore, when their strenuous efforts at reform were looked upon as the most uncalled-for and insupportable acts of aggression; when they were shunned as men stricken with the pest would have been; when they were accused of the most incredible fanaticism and socialism, and bemoaned by their friends and neighbours as being more left to themselves than drunkards, gamesters, or common thieves. Save the early Christians, no religious sect—not even the Reformers, whether Lollard or Lutheran—excited such a storm of hostility, or were so universally despised, detested, and reviled as were the followers of Wesley.

The young Squire of the Mall was so neglected and forsworn by his brother squires and the families of the better classes in the neighbourhood, that had it not been for his healthy, independent nature, and his great friendship for his father, he might have been driven into the low company to which Methodism was then generally believed to incline.

Old Squire Gage had been fortified against the deleterious and destructive consequences of such an atmosphere by such airs from heaven as visit few men's souls. It is not asserted here, however, that it had not injured him, developed oddities in him, sapped ever so little his simplicity and energy, and made him, notwithstanding all his benevolent projects, more of an abstract thinker and dreamer than a practical man.

But young Caleb Gage could hardly expect the same immunity; and it was well for him that he was not equally tried. In the public places which his principles did not forbid him to frequent, and in one or two neighbouring houses which, for ancient alliances' sake, still offered an open door to a Gage of the Mall, Caleb had some intercourse with his class, and was not so entirely proscribed, denounced, and doomed to live down his differences of creed and life as his father had been.

Thus it chanced that, happening to attend the yearly fair at Reedham, Caleb Gage supped and stayed for the night at the house of a tolerant Reedham physician, who had been his father's worthy doctor for the last half century. Doctor Humphrey was no Methodist himself, though he had accorded his evidence:

"I like to attend your patients at the Mall, Squire; for the most part they're patient as well as patients; and I'd liever wait on their death-beds than those of most others, for, however sorrily they live, they make up for it by dying well, they do—yes, your Methodists die well."

At Dr. Humphrey's, on this occasion, Caleb met, among other young people, Mr. Philip Rolle's daughters; and in the intervals between the games and the songs he had to submit to be stared at and tittered over, and viewed as a curiosity almost as great as the wild beasts they had visited at the shows in the afternoon. Mr. Caleb Gage had himself visited the wild beasts, and he had also gone and listened for a time to the Methodist preacher, whose stage was competing with the dancing booths, and had joined heartily in the hymn-singing; and when there had been a threatening demonstration in the crowd in that quarter, he had sprung up on the stage, and prepared to use his personal influence to ward off violence, and take his chance with the preacher and his friends.

Caleb was not without something of what Grand'mère would have called *la beauté du diable*—the morbid attraction of forbidden fruit to his detractors and assailants; and he had himself a half-amused perception of the fact, while he had no great inclination to return the compliment. The Methodist home was a different school of manners, to say the least of it; and these vapouring, swaggering young men, and swimming, bridling young women, appeared ruder-tempered and emptier-headed to Caleb than they would have appeared to his father, because Caleb as yet judged largely by the surface; while the old Squire had a poet's and a prophet's plumb-line to fathom many feet deeper into human nature.

There was one gibe constantly recurring

on the least provocation in sentiment, or forfeit, or game of the Traveller, and this was Caleb's supposed attachment to French fashions. The gibe was followed by taunting assertions that somebody's troth might have been sold in his cradle, and that he might have exchanged the pap-boat for the wedding-ring, so tame-spirited was he.

"My head is somewhat thick," admitted Caleb Gage to Dolly Rolle, at a crisis of the by-play. "I must confess that you distance me in your merriment. I cannot think what you are all driving at. When did I discover a palate for foreign kickshaws? (It is as clear as the sun that it is me you mean, so none need go to deny it.) As far as I can tell, my tastes are all English; for that matter, I have no chance of gratifying them otherwise, since I have not so much as the entrance to any strange circle, unless it be that of the French

Huguenot family at the Shottery Cottage in Sedge Pond, which my father esteems so highly."

Caleb did not observe, or else he paid no heed to Dolly's smiles, nods, and winks at his unlucky allusion.

"As to marriage," Caleb went on stoutly, "I presume I should have some inkling, if I were ever so little started on the road to the church on that solemn business; whereas, mistress, I have as little thought of marrying till I cut my wisdom-teeth as the black fellow behind your chair has of taking a white wife."

"If you speak so fast," answered Dolly, pertly, "I shall either think that it is part of your Methodist religion to swear down one's throat white is black; or else that you are the most deceived, misused young man who has ever been chosen a bridegroom without his consent asked."

"Think nothing of the kind, madam," replied Caleb, annoyed and indignant at her folly; "but tell me right out, if your high-church religion have the courage and the honesty to do so,—which, to be sure, I doubt not," he corrected himself, already ashamed of his recrimination. "What do people say of me? They must needs have little to busy themselves about when they tell cock-and-bull stories on so trumpery a subject?"

"They do say extraordinary things of you, good young sir," asserted Dolly, with a toss of her head; "they say, of a verity, that you are right-down affianced to your white-faced, moon-struck neighbour, Ma'mselle Yolande Dupuy, who, if she be not a Papist, is certainly a mystic, so unlike is she to the rest of her sex,—even to her wise Grand'mère, to whose apron-string she is pinned. I'd rather have had Grand'mère, sir; but you'll be pinned to her likewise all the same, if she and your cracked father have courted for you, and engaged you without so much as saying, 'By your leave.' But I suppose they hold you so good a psalm-singing boy that you have no mind or will of your own in the matter? But, surely, in common justice they will let you know before the banns be published, that you may not look sheep-faced or grow white about the gills before the whole parish. To have gotten the sack were nought to it."

Dolly had been crammed and prompted by sharper and more malicious rustic wits than her own, or she never could have accomplished all these smart hits; but the sense of this only galled and fired Caleb Gage's manliness and spirit the more.

"It is all an untruth, an absolute untruth, Mistress Rolle," he declared, quickly and positively, "so manifest and ridiculous a fabrication, that it puzzles me reasonable people should combine—not to credit it—that they cannot do—but to circulate it."

But even while he spoke there flashed across his memory the coincidences, not only that his father had that very morning sounded him as to his opinion of every member of the family at the Shottery Cottage, and had pressed him when his answers were careless and vague, but that the Squire had repeatedly of late taken occasion to recommend him to unite himself with another, and had dwelt wistfully on his own happiness in the wife whom he had lost, and endeavoured to ascertain how Caleb stood affected to such a change of condition. The young man had naturally thought the discussion uncalled for and premature, and had parried it, or been restive under it, as his temper led him. But now that these recollections flashed across his mind inopportunely, Caleb's brown face flushed, and he contracted his square brow and bit his lips.

"You are not angry with me, Mr. Caleb!" cried Dolly, shrugging her shoulders, and adding slily, "Men are not angry at mere idle reports, and this one is no fault of mine; I did not raise it. I had it from my mother, and she had it from head-quarters —from old Madam Dupuy, upon my life. Now, be as angry with me as you like; nobody can say that I can help it."

The result of the spiteful treachery committed at Dr. Humphrey's was that Caleb Gage was tempted for twenty-four hours to think that his father and the Methodists were right in abjuring worldly society, and that he, for one, would never enter it again. More than that, on the next occasion that Caleb passed through Sedge Pond, and conveyed a letter from his father to Grand'mère, he refused obstinately to alight and partake of a second breakfast, or even to sit for a moment and exchange greetings at the garden gate. And when, in course of time, Caleb encountered Grand'mère and Yolande at some little distance near the door of the parish church, he did all he could to avoid the encounter, turned his head, looked another way, and behaved in all respects like a person deeply affronted.

"Somebody has growed high and mighty all of a suddent," remarked Priscille, decisively; "I lay the young Squire of the Mall have got a flea in his ear. Sirrah! quotha, if that be your Methody humility in taking the first word of scolding, I would not give my head for the article; it seems to me it do come out of the same pot as ourn and parson's at the Rectory, after all."

"Adieu *paniers*, vintages are done with,"

murmured Grand'mère, sorrowfully. She was not so much offended as hurt at the smart received in the house of a friend, at trying in a wearisome struggle to dissever the wrong from the wrong-doer, to count old Squire Gage blameless, and to make allowance for the wilfulness and perversity of the young man. Grand'mère felt that she had made a grievous blunder; not in the step she had taken—that was quite in accordance with her best light and the customs of her fathers—but in the direction into which the step had carried her. She had been rash, inconsiderate of English habits and tones of thought. At the same time she trusted with all her good heart that this brave *garçon*, who had slighted her child, been offended by their gracious preference, and returned it with what in French eyes was little less than brutal rudeness and marked insult, might not, after all, prove reprobate. But she feared much that her early deprecation of the free footing on which he stood with his father was correct, and that the young man was in the first stage towards the blasted ruin of lawlessness and infidelity.

Yolande endured for a longer season the changing moods of the Rolle girls, who soon began to condole with her on the failure of her match, and this, too, in accents widely removed from the spirit of their unusual contentment with their own present lot and confident anticipations of good fortune in the future. Then Yolande went to Grand'mère in her room, stood before her, and looking up in her face, said,

"Grand'mère, I am yours to do with what you will. Nothing can alter that. You will always know it is so. It is our French interpretation of a child's obedience and devotion, and anything else to us is mockery. But tell me, Grand'mère, and do not call me insolent for asking it (because, see you, I have been brought up in this harsh England, and you yourself have bidden me consort with loud-spoken English girls), you have offered me to this young man, and he has rejected me—is it not so?"

Yolande spoke with scorn, but it sounded as if it was scorn of herself, and of no other.

"You put it in hard words, Yolande, which is to pour the drug into an ugly glass," remonstrated Grand'mère, mildly. "It suffices that there was a project of marriage thought of for you by your friends, which on thinking over a second time they have abandoned by mutual consent—yes, I will say that now. Does that harm you?"

"I do not know, I cannot tell," hesitated Yolande. "You had the right,—you would serve me with your own dear grey hairs. But oh! Grand'mère," burst out Yolande, hiding her face in a paroxysm of distress, "why would you marry me if you risked shaming me? Why would you marry me at all, thrusting me on some man who does not want me, to whom I should be a burden and a bugbear? Oh, Grand'mère! it feels like shame, hot shame, and cruel wrong."

"But, surely, this is morbid," Grand'mère rebuked her child, in a little displeasure and a great deal more anguish and dismay. "This is English spleen and mad pride, of which I used to accuse you in jest—foolish jest. Your mother was given in marriage; your grandmother before her. Think you not that their fathers and mothers looked about them and made false starts, *coûte que coûte*, before they fell on the right *parti?* Are you so much better than they?"

"I am no better, Grand'mère, I am not half so good. But why must you have me married?"

"You may be left alone any day, you must be one day; then what would become of you, my child? You would have bread enough to eat, that is true, but would the world leave you to eat it in peace? Would it not abuse and betray you? There are no retreats for the Huguenots even in France, there never was any but *aigue morte* and the prisons. Women may live single in England without injury or scandal; but I have not seen it,—it is not the way in our country. It is only that I have been a stupid old woman in your interests, *fifille*, and I am very sorry for it."

"Do not say that, Grand'mère. It is a trifle, a tuft of thistle-down, I mock at it.

There, I toss it from me and catch it again for my own amusement, don't you see? A man is free to have his choice, and his refusal breaks neither my neck nor my heart, though it throws a stone at me. Rest tranquil, Grand'mère. Let us return to our sheep, our lace, to what you were telling me of your pigeons, your herbs at home in Languedoc."

"It is well," said Grand'mère to herself; "it is but the girl's spirit which is wounded, her heart is mute like a little fish, sleeps as a *sabot*,—and so it should, till it wake up by her husband's side. Who would rouse and force it into life sooner?"

Ah! short-sighted Grand'mère, if Yolande's had been a mean, jealous, grasping temper, you might have been secure; Caleb Gage's repudiation and aversion would have done its work. But with the small value Yolande set upon herself, and the large value you taught her to put on Caleb Gage, teaching all the more effectual that it had no direct personal reference; the impressions which you had laboured to give to her of the young Squire's manliness, liberality, truth, and tenderness—impressions made on a surface altogether blank, and capable of lightly and rapidly receiving them, and weaving them into a young girl's pure, graceful dreams;—it seemed no more than natural to Yolande that Caleb Gage should have nothing to say to her, there was no flaw in his nobility on that account, since he had not made a single advance from which he had drawn back. It was just, it was almost right that he should not find her worthy, he would not be less a hero in the girl's magnanimous eyes because of that. And she felt, with a throb of generous thankfulness, that she was not so unworthy as that came to, though he might have pained and humiliated her, and mingled a single strain of loving despair in the original gravity and thoughtfulness of her youth.

Days passed over the Cottage, and Grand'-mère watched Yolande covertly and incessantly, and saw, under the fair front which the young girl was sedulous to preserve, that she was still abstracted, and only fitfully interested in what was passing around her. She was liable to flashes of feverish restlessness and flushes of bitter mortification, and she sighed long and sorely when she thought nobody heard her drawing those deep, sad breaths, which, it is not altogether a figure to say, drain the life blood from the heart. Grand'mère believed it was high time to interfere and speak to Yolande, to seek to probe the wound which she had helped to inflict, with purer fingers.

"Yolandette," she addressed the girl, lying wide awake in the hush of the night, with no light upon her but that of the pale moon and the dim lamp, "hide nothing from me; it is my due, for I have nursed you in my bosom, and if I have hurt you I have a double right to know all."

"To what good, Grand'mère?" pleaded Yolande; "you will but widen the breach between me and my old self, and increase the scandal."

"I will not; I, an old mother, will show you what is worth all the sorrow, and will bring you consolation."

"How can you, Grand'mère?" objected Yolande, incredulously and desperately. "There is consolation for great, splendid griefs, but not for a girl's weak, vain delusions, though they cause her to fret and pine for them. Consolation does not demean itself to such poor, common, childish trials as these. Let me be, Grand'mère; let me rather crush them down, beat them like a stone under my feet. Trust me, I am wiser than my elder in this."

"No, no, that is a villainous mode—a heathen mode. Consolation is heavenly; if it were not so, I grant you it would not stoop so low; and yet, without that royal condescension to the least and the silliest soul, it would not be big enough even for earth. Listen to me, Yolande: dost thou feel womanly betimes, and as the heavy price of thy womanliness, dost thou recognise thyself in the morning of thy day as 'a woman forsaken,' despised in thy youth? So thou art called, in the words of the Bible, which were not spoken to a low-born, tormented, embittered woman truly, but to the true Israel, the spiritual Church. Notwithstanding, there are the words and the figures, and what will you—that it was the sympathy of the stern old prophet which breathed through their marvellous tenderness, or that it was Another who put them into Isaiah's wild imagination and on the burning lips which the live coal had touched —Another, the Friend of publicans and sinners, and of weak women as well as strong men."

"Are there such words, Grand'mère?" whispered Yolande, stirred and softened with awe and emotion. "I have read the Bible every morning and every evening, like other Huguenot girls, but I never discovered them or took them to myself."

"Nay, nor do we ever, *ma mie*, till we want them, or the Spirit shine upon them, because the well of Scripture is deep; still, truth is at the bottom of the well, Yolande, waiting for us when we need it, if we will have it. Listen better, Yolande." The lamp was trimmed; Grand'mère took out her Rochelle Bible from beneath the pillow, fixed her glasses, and with her shrunk ivory finger turned over the yellow pages and pointed to the spot, producing more convincing effect, and one more in keeping with moral and spiritual powers than when she and Squire Gage had recourse to the *Sortes Biblicæ*.

"Fear not; for thou shalt not be ashamed: neither be thou confounded; for thou shalt not be put to shame: for thou shalt forget the shame of thy youth, and shalt not remember the reproach of thy widowhood any more.

"For thy Maker is thine husband; The Lord of Hosts is his name; and thy Redeemer the Holy One of Israel; The God of the whole earth shall he be called.

"For the Lord hath called thee as a woman forsaken and grieved in spirit, and a wife of youth, when thou wast refused, saith thy God."

"Grand'mère," said Yolande, quivering

with eagerness, "the remembrance is, oh! so sweet from the great Bridegroom. I shall hold up my head again; I shall look *him* in the face again, Grand'mère. I shall not mind how I am laughed at and lightly esteemed; I shall think that I am good for something since my foolish yearning heart is read by Him who numbereth the stars and calleth the roll of prophets and martyrs, and ordereth the march of empires and worlds."

CHAPTER X.

The Rolles of the Castle.

REEDHAM was one of those old-fashioned towns in which the gaol was the central ornament. The shops were low-browed, and not much better than hucksters' stalls; but there was the beauty of irregularity about the better class of houses, advancing and retreating as they did on the causeway, and showing genuine antique oriel windows and balconies, with occasional vines festooning and tinting afresh the red brick.

One day in early spring the Rector of Sedge Pond had occasion to ride into Reedham. Approaching the market cross, he could not help uttering an exclamation as he saw a large printed placard posted there, signed "Audrey Rolle." A considerable gathering of rustics and townspeople gaped round it.

"Hath my lady put the crown on her vagaries and her usurpation of a man's place by proposing to sit in Parliament herself?" mused the Rector. "Indeed, there remains only this, that she and the like of her have not tried; and, by my word, if they set their minds on it, neither king nor constitution will balk them. Alake! alake! what waste of high spirit and high heart is there, and what might not my lady Rolle have been and done, had she been born a man, and been set down in the shoes of Cornwallis, or Burgoyne, or Rodney, or Anson, or Sir Robert, or the Duke of Newcastle, or even of the Bishop of London, or he of Bath and Wells? As it is, all her wit doth not serve to keep her at home, abiding by her still-room and her needle, ruling her maids, and saying her prayers, like my simple wife and maids, who will be all agog at the mere thought of their patroness being in the country again."

The Rector was somewhat relieved, however, when he found that the address only called on the men of Reedham to be early at the poll, and vote for the Honourable George Rolle. It concluded with the words: "As a mother who has already given a son to her country, and as the just price of her loss, I call upon my friends and neighbours to elect his brother, my next son, as their fitting representative in Parliament."

" Glad am I that it is the Honourable George, and not herself, whom my lady proposes, though she is a great deal better man than he is," thought the Rector.

"And so she makes gain of her poor hero, even for the honour and advantage of the house and of her remaining sons. Would I thus make gain of the pure memory of my Philip? Nay, perish the thought of all that was earthly in our connection. Let him henceforth shine as a star in the firmament for me; and let me obey my Master's orders, look up to Him, and covet earnestly to die in harness, fulfilling the measure of my duty as my boy fulfilled his, and following the Captain of our salvation. Nevertheless, I am a Rolle; and I owe my best duty to my lady, who has been good and kind to me according to her light, and my support to the Honourable George, who I am assured will never set the Thames on fire, save by dawdling between London and Paris, and heaping together pretty things like a vain woman. Still, how these puny fine gentlemen do shake off their affectations and follies, and strip and fight like men in the senate, baling out and forcing back the roaring tide of loathsome bilgewater—anarchy, infidelity, and horrible confusion, like what has fallen out in His Majesty's colony of America, which threatens to become the grave of true loyalty and virtue, in spite of hecatombs of corpses and rivers of gore poured into it, my Philip's gallant body and generous blood among the rest."

The first sight Grand'mère and Yolande had of Lady Rolle was in the obscurity of a whirlwind of dust raised by her chariot and that of her son, as they drove past Sedge Pond to the Castle. But when once the family were lodged in their proper quarters, there was no longer any dimness or uncertainty about the fact of their presence. Everything was turned upside down for them, and every movement was thenceforth directed towards them. They were like the sun in the sky, drinking in and absorbing all the exhalations, and in their central power controlling the growth and progress of every living creature around them. From the Rector in his surplice to Deborah Pott between her water-pitchers, no one was exempt from the influence of the Quality.

Grand'mere at first tried to resist the spell, and in a fit of national spirit talked of the great peers of France, the provincial parliaments, the lieutenants of the king, and the governors of provinces, compared with whom this English family were mere titled gentry, with mortgaged acres, and no power except that derived from their seats in Parliament, where they most undauntedly voted to each other sinecure upon sinecure.

But Grand'mère changed her mind after she had witnessed the Rolles' rule for a week, and seen the demonstrations at the village and in the little church. The church was situated with a manifest respect to persons, inasmuch as it forced upon the village Christians a weary trudge through a miry byway; while the Castle Christians, who were not at the Castle above once in two years, and only filled two pews when they were all at home, commanded an easy road by a side door from the park. There was such a scene there as Grand'mère had never witnessed in Roman Catholic France, where the great dignitaries of the Church, which aspires to rule the earth, exacted homage and humility from rival dignitaries, temporal princes, and peers, and did not often brook any claims save their own at the gates of either their noblest cathedrals or their simple parish churches. It was another matter when Lady Rolle appeared in the porch of the church at Sedge Pond. She was attended by her maid, chaplain, physician, butler, and sometimes by one of her sons, who with his bodily eye would stare at the scraps of stained glass which he had often seen before, instead of looking with his mental eyes into Heaven, to which it was doubtful if his imagination had ever taken flight. Nay, he would audibly remark on a rusty iron sword on the monument of one of his forefathers, which would never pink armour or slash buff coat more, at the very moment when the priest was praying for the sword of the Spirit to pierce the souls of those present, and that of the son among them. When the Castle party issued from their own particular door, the worshippers, who had flocked out before them, divided right and left, uncovered their heads, and bowed down as before divinities; while the Rector in his cassock, and his wife and daughters in their sacques and hats, hastened to show a proper example of reverence to superiors. At that crowning testimony Grand'mère grew very thoughtful, and in place of undervaluing the Rolles of the Castle any longer, she called them a great institution, an ordinance of God, for good or for evil, according as it was used or abused.

Monsieur—an avowed time-server, notwithstanding his irony—bowed low before the men of the Castle when they came down to the village to see a cock-fight, or play a game at skittles, or make trial of their horses entered for Newmarket, in the presence of a crowd of obsequious helpers and hangers-on. These Rolles were not mere roystering country Quality—not men of many glaring sins and a few redeeming virtues, like the publicans and sinners of old. They were more dangerous and difficult subjects to deal with—men of the court and the town, men of wit and fashion, of taste and refinement. They were not so much men of strong passions as of overweening vanity, and its complement, cynicism. In their small hats and wigs, plain black ribands or white ties, they lounged, as if half asleep, in the approaches to the Castle, and only roused themselves to pick their slippered steps, and carry their little French poodles and Italian greyhounds carefully over the puddles; while they stood, took pinches of snuff, betted, laughed, swore, and contemplated enjoyably two barges running foul of each other on the river; for, just as the degenerate Romans patted and petted their gladiators, these affectedly squeamish, womanish men were very fond of supping on horrors.

Monsieur bowed still lower before my lady, who, as distinguished from my lord, swept along in such piled-up tissues, jewels, powder, and plumes as only the great ones of the earth could compass. She looked as if she had been born to wear them; and she never rested day or night, but with her marvellously fine fretted features and falcon look, was for ever pursuing some aim with headlong, devouring intentness, and the moment it was attained, setting out after some other object, no matter what, so that it was hers to be sought after and gained.

Madame, Yolande's mother, looked darkly at those privileged players in a pageant, and called them Ahabs and Jezebels, Herods and Herodiases, and poured forth denunciations of " baldness in place of well-set hair, and burning for beauty." Yolande, too, looking with open, unconscious eyes at the new and striking figures on the stage of her life, and shrinking from the mocking, irreverent, unbelieving light alike in the soft, sleepy eyes of the men, and the ardent eyes of the woman, was tempted to say to Grand'mère—

"Are they not like Vashti, grown old and worn, but never weary? Do these unflinching spirits ever weary, Grand'mère? or do they only wear and wear, until the good God break them, and take them brokenly to Himself, and make of them the spirits which constitute heroes and martyrs? And the men, Grand'mère, are they not so many Absaloms? I like them not. I like my lady, who is eager to make us fear her—so eager, that she would tread over the necks and the hearts of the people, and her own also, Grand'mère—her own also. The men are false and cruel in their sleekness; they would sacrifice others, but save themselves, such as they are; I know it—I feel it."

"Yes, until to-morrow with your knowledge and feelings," reproved Grand'mère, soberly and sadly. "Who made you a judge between this woman and these men, or between them and yourself? Better shut you up in a portfolio at once, Mademoiselle my judge, than suffer you to look abroad with rash, harsh eyes and tongue. 'By their fruits ye shall know them?' Yes, truly; but these are the brethren; even an Apostle had nought to do in judging those who were without. And what fruits have you gathered of this great Rolle family?"

"Well, Grand'mère, I see enough of their mincing airs every day; I can scarce look at them when I see them in the walks."

"Ah! my heart, do you believe the Lord, when He tells how hard it is to be rich? Do you ever—I do not say thank the Lord that you are not of the *haute noblesse*—that were the Pharisee's prayer—pray to Him on behalf of those poor souls of whom He said that it was as easy for a camel to go through the eye of a needle as for them to enter his kingdom? But when they do go through the eye of a needle, think you not they are such as are made rulers over ten cities? But we are as silly and selfish as the little birds towards the cats: we are unbelievers; and instead of praying for the rich and helping them, we envy them and go on hating and maligning them."

"Oh, Grand'mère!" cried Yolande, with a sharp, pained voice.

"Alas! it is true, my child, and the harsher our judgments the greater will be our condemnation! *Ma mie*, I think of a chapter in my Bible, and I try to show you a better way in which to regard these messieurs. See you how they stand to look at and admire a group of trees in the park, a herd of deer, the tower of the church from one point, and their own arcade from another. Nay, they can admire a pretty child of the village, so that she be clean washed for their inspection, and put not her finger in her mouth, or whimper and hint that she is thinly clad and coarsely fed, and so rub against their skins, and, as they say, dispel the illusion."

"Ah! yes, that is true; I have seen them," responded Yolande, thoughtfully.

"They have the sense of beauty, Yolande, and beauty is the gift of God. See you again how they caress their little dogs, and mourn when the Rosines and the Rosettes hang their heads or droop their tails. But that is unworthy of men who have the whole world of men and women to care for, you will tell me. Well, I cannot say as to that; for the great God cares for the brutes as well as for men and women, and so I do not understand that branch of the argument."

"But it seems only a waste of tenderness, Grand'mere."

"Yes, yes, I admit it is a waste of tenderness in those who have little of the commodity to spare. Still it is tenderness, and that is a nobler gift of God than beauty. And now I will tell you something that you see not (may you never see it!), but what the common voice says of the strange gentlemen. In their conduct to their women they are alternately savage and sweet. The most terrible wrongs, the most barbarous outrages, have been committed by strong brothers against weak sisters, as if the strong were demons; and then, again, they act as if the pitying angels had dispossessed the demons, and had not disdained to take up their abode for a season in the dishonoured dwellings. My simple one, it is not that this man or that woman is a sinner above all other sinners, but that the foundations of the world are out of order, and that all our pleasant springs are poisoned, our good gifts marred. We are all sinners, great and small, as opportunities have enabled us or grace prevented us. We are all sinners, and—God be praised!—one is our Saviour. Leave Him to judge, and judge thou no more."

Lady Rolle had only a faint impression of the Dupuys as being the foreign tenants of the Shottery Cottage. Madame Rolle of the Rectory and her girls spoke of them to the great lady, but, sooth to say, the great lady paid little heed to such speech, calling it, in her sarcastic phrase, the cackle of ignorant country geese. But Lady Rolle, when the living book was in her hands, read a man better than most readers, and esteemed Mr. Philip, her friend and kinsman, more than any man alive, though it must be confessed she showed it quite as often by vexing as by pleasing him. And when he actually spoke of the Dupuys not unfavourably, her ladyship took it into her head to pay them a visit. She had, of course, no notion but that she could do anything she liked at Sedge Pond, and be everywhere humbly received and meekly deferred to; and so she went about deranging everything like some powerful, semi-malignant fairy. Her ladyship walked straight into the Shottery Cottage one day —right into the sombre parlour, and sat down, in Madame Dupuy's chair, without invitation or leave. She caught a glimpse of Grand'mère as she was looking round her, quite prepared to domineer and to find fault before she should make up for her bad behaviour by showering upon the occupants her prodigal money and favours.

She jumped up instantly, begged Grand'-mère's pardon, and craved permission to call her, on the spot, a dear old friend. From that fresh starting-point Lady Rolle poured her winning, wonderfully idiomatic, though broken French into her listener's credulous ears, and conducted herself towards Grand'mère as an amiable fine lady, unique and exquisite in her amiability, no less than in her humours and vices.

Not that Lady Rolle ceased to be herself: she reflected on Grandmère's family just a little of her bland good-will. She said distinctly to Madame,

"My good creature, you detest me at first sight. Have I such a bad taste, then, in a recluse's mouth? So much the worse for you, because I can really do without your liking, unless you put my dear old friend here up against me; whereas I might have been of some service to you, and been at ease in offering you the run of the Castle gardens, dairy, dove-cot, and farm, all the year round; in putting a stop to the hob-nailed louts molesting you, and compelling the county to be civil to you. Reflect what you have lost by finding in me your *bête noire*, your *croquemitaine.*" Addressing herself coolly to Monsieur, she went on: "Sir, I shall have no scruple in being useful to you. If I mistake not, you understand the commerce of society. What will you take in exchange for permitting me to be intimate with your mother and your daughter? Do I not know that you will receive no injury from the words of a plain Englishwoman? You are too wise a man of the world. Is it not so?"

"Precisely, my lady; you comprehend perfectly the character of the *bourgeois* who is dying with the wish to make a market of everything, without the exception of mother and child. I shall ask my price—when I want it." So Monsieur met her challenge, raising his shoulders and showing his teeth.

And Lady Rolle told Yolande: " Child, I could be vastly fond of you, and carry you off, will he, nill he, to take the place of my last scarlet spider; for I am getting up a collection of monsters to outshine Margaret Cavendish's. I warn you, my good mother, that I worry all my friends' hearts out of their bodies to help me with strange beasts, now that I have done with Greek marbles. But, child, you are not all your grandmother. I spy your mother in your face; and, as you see, she and I no more take to each other than plaguey teeth to gritting sand. There, don't take the pet, you little fool; perhaps hers is all the honester nature for not agreeing with mine. After sinners themselves, only saints and angels can put up with sinners; don't you know that? Be thankful, at least, that your mother is not a sinner of the same stuff as the French mothers whom I have known were made of. What were they like? Bah! Painted goddesses, ready to tear out the eyes of their own daughters, making frights of them, outraging them, to keep them from stepping on the *tapis* with themselves. I thank my stars that I have only long lazybones and grinning buffoons of sons, lest I should have seen rivals in my daughters, and bitten and devoured my own flesh and blood. But if the mothers were no better than they should be, how did it happen that the grandames were too good for this bad world? Sure I cannot tell. My wise head will not crack riddles like nuts. Grand'mère, you are not vexed with me? Nay, then, I shall confess that I have been only in ill company, that to the gadflies all the poor midges figure as gadflies. Yes, yes, that is it; and the French mothers are without reproach, like the old mesdames— like charming, wise, witty De Sevigné, whom we all dote upon, down to that snarling dog, Rolle. You are her marrow, my dear, beautiful old goody! only what a pity that you are *bourgeoise* and Huguenot. Could you not be at least orthodox Catholic here, where it would not be a feather in your cap —quite the contrary; so that you would still have the comfort of contradicting everybody and continuing a martyr?"

"Pity that she is a Huguenot!—Be a Catholic!" gasped Madame. "Why does not the earth open and swallow her up? *Mon mari*, you stand by and hear your mother insulted, the faith mocked! Go; I had not thought you so wicked. Who is this *scaramouche* of a De Sevigné? I know her not; I abjure her, for the company she keeps."

"Ah! be quiet, my good woman," enjoined Lady Rolle, tranquilly; "I do not mind you, De Sevigné does not mind you. Alas! she has only existed for us in her likeness this half century and more. But it is refreshing to find man or woman who believes anything, and who is not to say rude in her faith."

Lady Rolle curtseyed politely to Madame (who turned her back with an exasperated mow), tapped the reluctant Yolande under the chin, kissed the hand of Grand'mère, and presented her own hand to Monsieur, with the most ineffable air of condescension, to be led to her chariot, which was standing there in its empty splendour, mobbed by the people of Sedge Pond.

That very afternoon Lady Rolle sent her own serving-man and woman with hampers of red Burgundy and white Hermitage, baked meats, and fruits, along with the last fashions and working-materials, to Grand'-mère; thus overpowering the least mercenary but the most grateful spirit in the world. Madame, however, put her hands doggedly behind her back, and refused to touch the unclean thing. With the hampers came a little note, which began with an apology for her handwriting (she never could write, my lady said), and requesting permission to wait upon Grand'mère, and to bring her dish of tea with her, any time she could spare from the great business of the election, which she was to set agoing the next week. She was shocking bad company herself, and was but poorly supplied with any other up at the Castle; she had no stomach for the dull, conceited country gentry, though she would not have said that for a pension just then. What she would like, would be to gossip by the hour about her dear, delightful Madame de Sevigné.

Madame de Sevigné was the key to Grand'mère's charm for Lady Rolle, just as Fletcher of Madeley had been the key to her attraction for the old Squire of the Mall. In the teeth of the old, bitter grudge against the French, which the middle and the lower classes were given to cherish as being patriotic, the Quality had not only the strong tendency to Gallic fashions of which young Caleb Gage was unjustly accused, but they had a great rage for one wonderfully endowed woman, whose Christian virtues and heathen insensibility, in the midst of the depravity of the Court air she breathed, they were equally incapable of measuring and appreciating. Nevertheless, Les Rochers, the Tour de Sevigné, the hôtel at Paris, the château in Provence, were household words; the stately and picturesque figures which had once moved there were treasured shapes; while the unapproachable tender grace and *naïveté*, the keen shrewdness and ripe knowledge of the world—all indeed but the fervent, devout heart which the touch of moral pitch could not defile—were in that generation laboriously and affectedly mimicked in the meretricious correspondence of supercilious critics, arrogant men of letters, and statesmen as venal as they were powerful.

Grand'mère's world was infinitely wider, fresher, and more wholesome than that of her daughter-in-law. Grand'mère knew and eagerly acknowledged the sweet though strangely surrounded flower of French quality. At the same time, Grand'mère paid the penalty of her freer range. She did not see so clearly as Madame Dupuy did within her narrow limits. The elder woman was somewhat mystified and carried away by the homage offered—not to herself, but to her representative countrywoman. And she, in her turn, began to descant to Yolande on Madame de Sevigné. She talked with enthusiasm of the bright, beautiful, loving, charitable, pious grandame, who, in the midst of abounding iniquity, remained faithful at every stage of her long life—true wife, fond mother, devoted friend; who retired to solitude, and prayed in lowly abasement, who succoured the poor with her own gentle hands, and who, in running from all the stilted glory and stereotyped gaiety among which her lot was cast, retired not merely to her hayfields, her bouquets of roses, and her portraits of her daughter, but to sick-beds, from which direly infectious and deadly maladies drove craven priests and doctors, where she nursed the bodies and ministered to the souls of suffering humanity, till the last sufferer who was to be relieved by her rose from bed, and saw the honoured, aged kinswoman take her place and die in her stead. Grand'mère called Madame Sevigné the Gamaliel who stood between the Jews and the Christians; and, had she been well acquainted with English history, she might have called her heroine the John Evelyn who formed the link between the Cavaliers and the Puritans.

END OF THE FIRST VOLUME.

LONDON : PRINTED BY MACDONALD AND TUGWELL, BLENHEIM HOUSE.

www.ingramcontent.com/pod-product-compliance
Lightning Source LLC
Chambersburg PA
CBHW030732230426

43667CB00007B/685